Camellias

Printed in Singapore

for the publishers
B.T. Batsford Ltd
583 Fulham Road
London
SW6 5BY

ISBN 0 1734 7993 0

A catalogue record for this book is available from the British Library

Photographs by Michael Lishman:
Front cover
Back cover 'Joan Trehane'
p 13 'C.M. Hovey'
Pg 19 'Donation'
Pg 22 'E.G. Waterhouse'
Pg 23 Supplied by Descanso Gardens, California

All others by the author

Line drawings by Shaun Le Gassick

Camellias

The Complete Guide to their Cultivation and Use

Jennifer Trehane

B.T. BATSFORD LTD, LONDON

Acknowledgements

Many thanks are due to my father, David Trehane, whose inspiration and guidance has been behind everything; to Bob Cherry at Paradise Plants in Australia, who read my first 20,000 words for me and gave me much frank and valuable advice at that stage. Thanks also to my son, David, who taught me how to use a computer, and has been a model of patience and a great moral support, also linguist daughter Penny, who corrected much poor English, and professional photographer son-in-law, Mike Lishman who took the cover photograph and some of the individual blooms within the book. Grateful thanks too to international plant nomenclature expert, my cousin Piers Trehane, who corrected my mistakes in plant nomenclature and to Professor Xia Lifiang and Guan Kayan from the Kunming Institute who put up with a constant stream of requests for information while travelling in Yunnan and Sichuan, not forgetting all the many friends and colleagues, especially within the ICS and the Camellia Societies of New Zealand, California and Australia, who have given so freely of their time and knowledge, as well as allowing me to take photographs in their gardens.

Last but not least, thanks to Janina Godowska, my editor at B.T. Batsford, especially for her patience and calmness.

CONTENTS

INTRODUCTION

Camellias have been appreciated in their native lands in southeast Asia, particularly in China and Japan, for perhaps 5,000 years, initially for their economic value as producers of both tea and oil, and later for the great beauty of their flowers. Their recorded distribution to the rest of the world has only taken place during the last 260 years, with first seeds, then plants reaching Europe then America and Australia, followed by New Zealand and South Africa. Some of the more fascinating stories from the history of the spread of camellias worldwide have been included here.

There have been ups and downs as fashions changed or political or social situations eclipsed their importance of diverted interest Since the discovery of more species in the wild and the breeding of varieties which were hardier or more sun-tolerant and therefore more versatile than at first believed possible they have greatly increased in popularity. The supply of both good garden and good show varieties has really taken off since the 1940s, with over 32,000 listed in the *International Camellia Society Register* and more in the *Supplement*. More people than ever before are discovering the joy of camellias and the pleasure they can bring to a garden, yard, terrace or conservatory.

It is said that the best way to learn is to teach, to which might be added that the best way to learn about camellias is to run a specialist nursery. Anyone who does so will be familiar with the constant stream of phone calls and letters, not to mention flowers and leaves in varying stages of decay, which arrive from customers or potential customers asking for indentification or guidance. It is rewarding work to find the answers to these queries. The author has been fortunate to have been, for a number of years, in charge of the specialist camellia nursery started by her father in southern England, and particularly since ceding control to her brother in December 1994, has travelled widely (Australia, China, New Zealand, the USA, South Africa and France, with just nine hours so far in Japan), as an ethusiastic student of the genus *Camellia*, and as an active member of the International Camellia Society.

The results of these studies are encapsulated in this book, which , hopefully, covers most of the 'why, where and how to's' of growing camellias in most climates, with perhaps more of the 'whys' explained in plain English, than are covered in most books of this type It does not pretend to cover all aspects in details; for example, potential hybridisers will to find information about the generic aspects of camellia breeding; no chromosome counts or compatibility tables. This aspect is in a state of rapid change, as much work is being done on DNA analysis and further morphological study, and it was felt that it should be left out at this stage. In any case, most of the best varieties are the result of the work of the bees!

Dedicated camellia show experts will not find any secret formulae; there are as many of these as there are exhibitors, but there are hints to point the way for those who wish to get started on this sociable hobby.

Joining a camellia society, visiting gardens, nurseries and camellia shows all add to the pleasure, and there are lists of some of these as well as a descriptive list of just a few (about 200) of the cultivars currently available for purchase.

This is essentially a practical book, written by a practical person and it is hoped that it will encourage others to share with the author an enthusiasm for a most fascinating and rewarding genus.

1

The History of Camellias as Garden Plants

Probably the most important camellia species is *Camellia sinensis*. It has been appreciated since the flavour of an infusion of its leaves was discovered around 5,000 years ago. Most of us enjoy a cup of tea, or 'cha', without realising that we are drinking camellia 'juice'! The origins of tea drinking are lost in the mists of time and Chinese folklore, but one of the popular tales taken from the eighth century 'Ch'a Ching' or 'Tea Classic' tells how in 2737 BC the Emperor Shen Nung was watching boiling water in an open kettle when leaves from an overhanging tree fell into it. He liked both the aroma and the taste, and the infusion from leaves of the tree, now identified as *camellia sinensis*, became popular from that time to the present. With its original royal associations, it is not surprising that the now famous Tea Ceremony evolved both in China and in Japan. Tea, either as unfermented green tea leaves, or brown, fermented leaves, or even compressed into a brick, travelled well

and spread throughout the world, arriving in England in the late 16the century. Thus the first camellias arrived in Europe. The other form in which camellias have for centuries been appreciated is in the form of oil, extracted by crushing the seeds. This oil comes from any camellia species growing in the locality which sets fruit regularly and easily. It has been used mainly for cooking, but also as a hair oil. In China it is *Camellia oleifera* which is so widely distributed both in the wild and under cultivation, while in Japan *Camellia sasanqua* is the dominant species and is most widely used for oil production. *Camellia reticulata* and several more species are also used, but the industry is in decline as other, more manageable crops such as oil seed rape and sunflowers take over.

Camellias have been growing and flowering in the wild, over a wide area of Southeast Asia, particularly in China, since time immemorial, of little interest to the majority of the subsistence farmers whose survival left no time for aesthetics. It was the temple priests who are accredited with the first appreciation and interest in the cultivation of camellias for their ornamental value. The Buddhist love of brightness and colour brought selections from the surrounding countryside into the temple gardens and courtyards, and the first cultivated, named varieties were undoubtedly the result of these selections and subsequent deliberate crosses. As the migrations of priests from one area to another extended, so did the spread of camellias, both as seeds and probably as plants. Wealthy landowners enjoyed their gardens too, and they, like the priests, valued their camellias, not just for their beauty and for spiritual refreshment but also as symbols of status and wealth. It is significant that throughout all the many feuds and hardships of China's tempestuous history, many of the oldest ornamental camellia trees have somehow survived. There are several over 250 years old and one or two of 500 years or more. There are even some claiming to be over 1,000 years old; probably either regrowths from ancient stumps, or the result of local enthusiasm and a desire to please western tourists.

Japan, with two important and highly ornamental native camellia species of its own (C. *japonica* and C. *sasanqua*), has, for centuries, had religious and trade links with China, and developed camellia growing for pleasure to a fine art. This, coupled with an accompanying mysticism, enabled a comprehensive list of cultivars to be available in Japan by the end of the 16the century. Most of these were from C. *japonica* or its forms.

CAMELLIAS ARRIVE IN EUROPE

Britain

The popular view, at least in Britain, where evidence is supported by written records, is that Lord Petrie of Thorndon Hall in Essex, England, was known to have a flowering camellia plant of what appears to have been C. *japonica*, in 1745. We do not know if it was imported as a live plant or raised from seed, but it was certainly a well established specimen by that year when the artist George Edwards painted his stylised illustration of a *Peacock Pheasant from China* sitting on what has been identified, more from the written description (which tells us that it was an evergreen with glossy leaves) than the picture, as a flowering branch of a camellia. Edwards states that he did the picture 'from Nature', using Lord Petrie's plant, which was amongst a much larger collection of exotics.

Other camellias were undoubtedly tried in the next 50 years, but the first named varieties to attract attention were C. *japonica* 'Alba Plena' and C. *japonica* 'Variegata' which were brought to England by Captain Connor on the British East India Company's ship *Carnatic* in 1792. From then on other named varieties such as C. *japonica* 'Rubra Plena' in 1794, C. *japonica* 'Incarnata' (also known as 'Lady Hume's Blush'), in 1806 and C. *japonica* 'Fimbriata' in 1816 followed as camellias became more fashionable. The trouble was that they were being grown, along with other 'exotics', in overheated 'stove' houses, which were not only hot, but humid, and many of them died.

This did not stop enterprising nurserymen such as Alfred Chandler of Vauxhall, London, from raising several new varieties, including C. *japonica* 'Chandleri' in 1825 and the much

The Camellia House at Wardour Castle, Wiltshire, England. Built as an orangery in 1769, probably first used for camellias early in the 19th century, when its tiled roof was replaced with glass

better *C. japonica* 'Elegans' in 1831. He was probably encouraged by the report by Samuel Curtis in the July 1814 edition of the *Botanical Magazine* which tells how 'a variety of *C. japonica* with single red flowers... is found to be hardy enough to bear being exposed during winter in the open air'. This made people realise that camellias were happy in cooler conditions and perhaps made astute nurserymen realise that there would be an increase in the potential market for camellias if they could be grown in gardens by all and sundry instead of needing the protection of expensive glasshouses which only the rich could afford. *C. japonica*' Elegans' is popular worldwide as a hardy garden camellia to this day.

Chandler's catalogue of 1825, titled *Camellia Britannica*, lists several other seedlings raised by Alfred Chandler. Others are reported to have been exhibited in London in 1824 and 1825. Camellia breeding had well and truly begun in Britain but relatively few of the early *japonicas* proved satisfactory outdoors except in the warm micro-climates of gardens

The restored Camellia House at Chiswick House, London

C.j. 'Elegans' at Chiswick House

in London and in Cornwall.

The Victorian age was a golden era when special camellia houses were constructed by the wealthy to house their prized plants. The famous example, designed by Joseph Paxton (famed for his design for the Crystal Palace for the Great Exhibition of 1851) was the special camellia house constructed for the Duke of Devonshire, at Chatsworth House in Derbyshire, England, to house the two plants of *C. reticulata* 'Captain Rawes' and one of *C. japonica* 'Alba Plena' planted in 1840. They are still healthy and bloom prolifically each spring in the same house.

Another, larger camellia house, also built by Paxton for the same Duke of Devonshire, is at Chiswick House in southwest London, where the collection includes *C. japonica* 'Variegata', *C. japonica* 'Incarnata', *C. japonica* 'Alba Plena' and some fine specimens of *C. japonica* 'Elegans' amongst others.

Eaton Hall, owned by the Duke of Westminster, also boasts a magnificent, long, narrow Camellia House which houses a splendid collection. Although many of the old plants have, unfortunately, gone, many more recent, choice varieties have been planted to fill the gaps.

The craze for camellias was not confined to England, but spread rapidly to continental Europe and to the USA, Australia, New Zealand and South Africa during the 19the century.

Portugal

Much discussion followed a report in 1959 that the family archives of the Conde de Campo Bello tell of three camellias being planted in the garden of the Villa Nova de Gaya in Oporto, Portugal in 1550. This seems a likely story, because the Portuguese were in Japan in 1542 when one of their ships was shipwrecked there, and there was certainly active trade between Japan and Portugal between 1549 and 1639. However, the origin of these plants has been vigorously denied by historians and by family descendants who claim that the first camellias were brought into the Oporto area between 1808 and 1810. Only carbon dating, which would involve taking a core from the trunk of one of the trees, would settle the issue.

There are many other old camellias in this area, and it is known that Portuguese nurserymen were actively introducing new varieties during the latter part of the 19the century. One nursery listed 665 varieties in his 1887 catalogue, 161 of them Portuguese bred. They seem to have gone in for long names; *C. japonica* 'Augusto Leal de Gouveia Pinto' (1904) still attracts attention on the show benches today, as does the later *C. japonica* 'Dona Herzilia de Freitas Magalhaes', (1949). No new varieties of any significance have emerged from Portugal in recent years.

Italy

C. sasanqua was recorded growing in the Royal Palace gardens at Caserta in 1760, according to Berlese writing in 1837. He also lists 282 varieties of *C. japonica*. Camellias were collected with enthusiasm, with one doctor, Luigi Sacco, having 12,000 camellias in his collection in 1830. Camellia breeding began early in Italy, with hundreds of new varieties, mostly of *C. japonica*, being introduced and sold throughout Europe in the next 50 years. Striped varieties were extremely popular. *C. japonica* 'Lavinia Maggi', formerly *C. japonica* 'Contessa Lavinia Maggi', the well known formal, double white-striped with carmine, dates from 1858. *C. japonica* 'Bella Romana', which dates from the same period, is still widely grown in Europe, although it fails to flower freely outdoors in Britain, as do many of the early Italian introductions. Its large pink flowers with crimson stripes are glorious in warm climates and pathetically small in cold areas.

Italian nurseries have specialised in growing fields of camellias to large 'specimen' sizes for many years. They are kept pruned to a tidy, appealing shape and are eventually dug up, containerised in huge tubs and sold in London and elsewhere to those who require 'instant' gardens.

France

In 1819 l'Abbé Berlese moved from the monastery of Sainte-Rose in Italy to Paris, as chaplain to the French Court, taking with him camellia seed from Caserta, from which he raised 100 plants. Here, he developed his lifelong interest in camellias and published three editions of his *Monographie du Genre Camélia* between 1837 and 1845. His three-volume *Iconographie du Genre Camélia* appeared between 1841 and 1843 with 300 illustrations. He finally disposed of his substantial camellia collection in 1846 and moved back to Italy where he died in 1863.

In the mid-19the century camellia corsages and buttonholes became popular, and camellia

Reputed to be the oldest camellia in France, *C.j.* 'Latifolia' in the cemetery at La Trinité, between Quimper and Nantes in Brittany

a wonderfully outrageous advertisement for camellias.

At this time 491 camellia plants were exhibited at the Concours Annuel des Camélias in Luxembourg, and the Guichard camellia nursery was founded in Nantes. The varieties *C. japonica* 'Gloire de Nantes' and 'Ville de Nantes' (a sport of *C. japonica* 'Donckelaeri') were bred here, and camellias from this nursery were despatched all over Europe and even to Argentina and Uruguay. The Jardins des Plantes just opposite the railway station in Nantes has made strenuous efforts to maintain a collection of the historic camellias.

Belgium

In 1809 two red camellias, probably *C. japonica*, were entered in the Ghent Flower Show, and in 1820 there were 44 entries. *Camellia reticulata* varieties were recorded in Belgium in 1825 and by 1850 J. Balmain of Ghent listed over 700 varieties, mostly *C. japonica* cultivars, in his catalogue! In 1830 Van Siebold brought a subsequently very well known *C. japonica* cultivar back from China, under its Chinese name. It was renamed 'Donckelaeri' after a well respected Belgian plantsman, and has proved to be very hardy and popular, despite the fact that its red and white, blotched flower colours are due to virus infection. He was lucky to receive this plant as most of his shipment was destroyed by rampaging French cavalry horses in Antwerp which was being besieged by the French at the time. This variety later achieved fame as one of the parents of *C. x williamsii* 'Donation'. *C. japonica* 'Tricolor' was another camellia saved from this melee and named by Andre Donckelaer.

plants were even sold in the street markets. *La Dame aux Camélias*, based on the Parisienne courtesan Marie du Plessis, was immortalised by Alexandre Dumas, with her famous bouquets of red or white camellias, depending on the time of the month, displayed prominently in her 'box' at the Opéra along with her packet of sweets. It was a pity she died of consumption at the age of 23; she was

Germany

Probably the most famous German camellia is the one planted in the palace gardens at Pillnitz in 1801, and still flowering with the benefit of the protective housing which covers it in winter. It is said to have come from England in 1771. In 1813 Siedel moved to Dresden from Paris, and by 1840 he was growing over 100,000 camellias under glass, and the nursery, by 1890, listed about 1,000 cultivars, mostly of *C. japonica*, in its catalogue. Plants were exported all over Europe and to Russia.

Interest in camellias declined in Europe towards the end of the 19the century. This appears to have been due to a mixture of factors, not least the natural cycle of changes in fashion. They had been a great craze and, like all crazes, it came to an end and gardening enthusiasts moved on to other things. Social and political changes were taking place too. Few people realised that some camellias could be grown outdoors, and so many of the varieties at that time had been raised in the warm climates of Portugal, Italy and Brittany, or in glasshouses elsewhere in Europe, and were only suited to these conditions. The Industrial Revolution, which had been responsible for generating so much wealth, had come to an end, and the number of landowners who had previously been able to staff and maintain large glasshouses gradually declined. Political strife in Europe, particularly the Great War of 1914–1918, and the Depression of the late 1920s and early 1930s, accelerated this decline. Times were hard, and few people had the inclination, the time or the money to bother with what were regarded as 'exotica'.

C.j. 'C.M. Hovey', an early introduction from Massachusetts, USA, named after its breeder, dates from 1850

CAMELLIAS WORLDWIDE

America

The first ornamental camellia to arrive in America was a single red *C. japonica*, landed in New Jersey, from England in 1797 or 1798, imported for John Stevens by a New York State nurseryman called Michael Floy who added a 'double white' (*C. japonica* 'Alba Plena'?) in 1800. Seventeen varieties were listed in a New York catalogue in 1822, 39 in another in 1835. Their popularity spread and by 1829 the Massachusetts Horticultural

Society was featuring camellias in its show.

From these early imports camellias spread to the warmer west coast, and to the deep south where the wealthy plantation owners were able to establish large collections in their gardens from the 1830s onwards. It was still, however, in the more highly populated and industrial northeastern States where, as in Europe, glasshouses were used to protect the plants, that activity was at a peak. A group of camellia enthusiasts in Boston are thought to have imported most of the available European varieties of the day between 1830 and 1860. The nurseryman C.M. Hovey of Boston was extremely active in promoting camellias and the red formal double variety C. japonica 'C.M. Hovey', which is still on virtually every nursery list, is a fitting memorial to him. Philadelphia was also a major centre of interest. Although there was a temporary lull in interest during the Civil War, it picked up in the early years of the century. Sacramento was named 'Camellia City' in 1910 and held its first show in 1924. By the 1930s camellia shows were being held in eight States, and the Azalea and Camellia Society of America, later to merge with the American Camellia Society, was formed in 1932.

Australia

The first camellias arrived in Australia from England on the SS *Sovereign* in February 1831, sent by John Macarthur junior to his sister Elizabeth and brothers James and William at the family estate, Camden Park, New South Wales. They included the ubiquitous C. *japonica*, and C. *japonica* 'Alba Plena' and also, the anemone form 'old Waratah camellia' now known as C. *japonica* 'Anemoniflora'.

This old Chinese variety (named 'Baozhu Cha', meaning 'Precious Pearl Camellia' in China) originally brought into England in 1806, is probably the first anemone-form camellia to be used in camellia breeding .With all its stamens petaloid and therefore with no pollen available, it was used by William Macarthur as a seed parent. He raised four or five hundred seedlings, mostly from this plant, and named 69 of them. Most have been lost, maybe because they were, curiously, propagated by layering, instead of the more secure grafting. C. *japonica* 'Aspasia Macarthur', a white peony form with a pink flush at the base of the petals, raised in 1848, is still grown.

Camellia popularity escalated in Victorian times, with Michael Guilfoyle sweeping the board at the Sydney Camellia Show in 1856. Nearly 2,000 camellias were exhibited at this event. Guilfoyle was both a nurseryman and camellia breeder. His large rich, pink formal double, C. *japonica* 'Jouvan', is still grown in Australia. T.W. Shepherd was another prominent breeder and nurseryman of the time. His lovely red anemone form C. *japonica* 'Speciosissima', introduced in 1862, and his peony form C. *japonica* 'Azurea', which is deep red, or purple in some soils, are both still around.

The Camellia Grove nursery at Paramatta, probably the first of its name, was founded in 1852 by Silas Sheather, who developed his interest in camellias while working for the Macarthur family at Camden Park. (The present, excellent, Camellia Grove nursery has different origins and is at St Ives, Sydney.)

Alexander Hunter was another camellia breeder of the Victorian age, with the glowing red semi-double *japonica* variety, named after him in 1941, still grown all over the world. His final home on the edge of Mangrove Mountain at Somersby, near Gosford, NSW, only has a few of his camellias left – just a small thicket of tall, neglected unnamed seedlings remain today.

The most famous and certainly the most venerated Australian camellia personality has to be Professor Waterhouse (1881-1977) whose home and garden at Eryldene, Gordon, in the northern suburbs of Sydney are now administered by a Trust. His *williamsii* hybrids all resulted from the acquisition of a plant of *C. saluenensis* from the British nursery Scott of Merriott in Somerset, which he only had from 1938 to 1946 when it perished from 'die-back' (*Glomerella cingulata*). All these varieties were selected from the 22 seedlings which the Professor dug up from under his *C. saluenensis* plant, and were the result of fertilisation by pollen from surrounding camellias which are varieties of *C. japonica*.

The Professor was also one of the founders of the International Camellia Society and, in 1952, of the Australia and New Zealand Camellia Research Society.

Camellias declined in popularity in Australia from the end of the 19th century and only regained their popularity in the 1940s.

New Zealand

The date of the arrival of the first camellias in New Zealand is not certain, but it appears that they arrived with some of the missionaries and the major source of supply seems to have been the Macarthur garden at Camden Park, NSW, Australia. Some very old plants have been found on the sites of abandoned mission station gardens on North Island; the oldest possibly being planted in 1834 at Mangapouri on the Punui river. Those at Ardmore on the Wairoa river and in the Makikiri river valley all date from the 1880–1895 period and include varieties bred in Australia. The catalogues of 19the-century nurserymen in New Zealand date back to the William Hale of Nelson

Professor Waterhouse's home and garden at Eryldene, Sydney, are now administered by a Trust

C.j. 'Donckelaeri', the pollen parent of *C.* x *williamsii* 'Donation'

catalogue of 1861, which lists nine varieties, including C. *japonica* 'Imbricata Alba', C. *japonica* 'Aspasia', C. *japonica* 'Peoniflora'. All nurseries list varieties collected from European sources (which included some varieties imported to England from China and given English names) and from the Macarthur nursery in Australia. By 1870 camellias were extremely popular in New Zealand, with one gardener reporting 70 different varieties in his garden in the Hutt valley, probably all imported from Australia. By the end of the 19th century there were about 250 varieties for sale in the country as a whole.

The popularity of camellias does not appear to have declined in New Zealand until the 1920s.

RECENT HISTORY

The *williamsii* story

The revival in interest in camellias throughout the world started in the mid-1930s, but did not really take off until after the second World War ended in 1945.

In England it was the collection of seeds of *C. saluenensis* in China by the plant hunter George Forrest which has had the greatest influence. He was commissioned by the Edinburgh Botanic Gardens, with additional financial help from various interested private garden owners. He made two collections of *C. saluenensis* seed between 1917 and 1919, four in 1924 and one in 1925 (Sealy). These were distributed to various sponsors, including the Williams family of Caerhays Castle in Cornwall. They owned five properties, one of which was Greenway, near Brixham, Devon, which was subsequently owned by the crime novelist Agatha Christie. Others included Werrington Park, near Launceston, Burncoose, near Camborne, Trewidden near Penzance, and of course, the family seat at Caerhays Castle near St Austell, Cornwall. Other seeds were sent to, amongst others, George Johnstone of Trewithen in Cornwall, Colonel Stephenson-Clarke at Borde Hill in Sussex, and to Edmund de Rothschild at Exbury, Hampshire. Lieutenant Colonel Messel exhibited flowers from his seedling, under Forrest's collection number 24090 (the same as one of the collections from which John Charles Williams received seeds) and was duly awarded an Award of Merit at the Royal Horticultural Society in London in 1930.

These wild *C. saluenensis* seeds produced plants with as much variation in their flowers as in the wild, as might be expected. The Exbury seedlings included one with deep pink, scented flowers, while both Caerhays and Borde Hill had forms which were both very pale pink.

It was found that *C. saluenensis* flowered at a very young age, as early as two years from sowing, and also set seed very readily, so hybridisation was possible relatively soon after arrival in this country. J.C. Williams used one of his pale pink *C. saluenensis* seedlings as the seed parent onto which he introduced pollen from a white *C. japonica* flower. This was done, according to J.C. Williams's grandson Julian, in about 1923. The details are lost to us because J.C. Williams's detailed records were in his briefcase which was stolen, together with £50, while he was travelling on the overnight train to London. A number of seedlings were raised from this cross, one of which, 'J.C. Williams', was named after its originator. It was first brought to the attention of the public in an article by Lord Aberconway in an *RHS Journal* of 1940 and was awarded a First Class

A pale pink form of *Camellia saluenensis,* like the seed parent of 'Donation' (photographed in the wild in Yunnan)

Certificate in 1942.

Others in the original series, all named before J.C. Williams's death are 'St Ewe', 'November Pink', 'Charles Michael' and 'Mary Christian'. The last one has broader leaves than would be expected and is more vigorous; in fact more like a *C. japonica* cultivar in many ways, and some doubt has been cast as to its place in this group. All are excellent garden plants and J.C. Williams has been rewarded posthumously because his name is now recognised worldwide as we now call all *C. saluenensis*/*C. japonica* crosses: *williamsii* hybrids.

More widely grown than 'J.C. Williams' is *C. x williamsii* 'Donation', raised at Colonel Stephenson Clarke's garden at Borde Hill in Sussex by his head gardener, Walter Fleming. He used the old *C. japonica* 'Donckelaeri' as the pollen parent on one of the pale pink flowered forms of the Forrest collected *C. saluenensis*, to produce a number of seedlings, from which 'Donation' was selected. This was probably in 1928, but 'Donation' was not brought to the attention of the public until it was awarded an 'Award of Merit' in 1941. Like 'J.C. Williams', it flowers incredibly prolifically over a long period but it has larger flowers and better leaves. It also grows more quickly in the early years, which makes it more commercial in the nursery trade.

Other *williamsii* hybrids were produced by other breeders – notably 'Francis Hanger' and 'Golden Spangles' from the RHS garden at Wisley, 'Hiraethlyn' from Bodnant in north Wales, 'Mildred Veitch' from the famous, now defunct, Veitch nursery at Exeter, and the interesting 'C.F. Coates' raised at Kew by using pollen from a *C. japonica* which had fishtail leaves, on *C. saluenensis*. 'C.F. Coates' has a simple pink flower like its *saluenensis* parent and fishtail leaves from its *japonica* parent.

What also became apparent very quickly as they were distributed throughout the country, was that all these hybrids were able to withstand cold winters better than *C. saluenensis*, but flowered more freely than the vast majority of cultivars of *C. japonica* then available. They combined the good points of

Bred by Les Jury in New Zealand 'Anticipation'

both parents while their less desirable features were more or less eclipsed. An added bonus was the ability of most of them to be self-grooming – they shed their flowers as soon as they are spent.

The war years intervened and it was not until some prosperity returned and people were able to divert their attention from vegetable growing to ornamentals once more that camellias began to be planted in gardens again. The social change to more home ownership, and the security and permanence this brings, also had an effect when considering the purchase of plants which are of long-term benefit and considered relatively expensive.

My father, David Trehane, must take credit for his work in popularising camellias in Britain during the 1960s and 1970s. He and I started the family nursery near Wimborne in Dorset in 1959 to grow blueberry plants for our new blueberry fruit enterprise. After

'Señorita'

'Jury's Yellow'

C. x williamsii 'Donation', the most popular camellia for
colder climates

my marriage and move to East Anglia he decided to concentrate on camellias and collected a huge assortment from all over the world. One of the breeders with whom he made contact was Les Jury from New Plymouth in New Zealand who has been responsible for producing more successful *williamsii* hybrids than any other breeder. My father became his agent and as each numbered seedling arrived (as a small unrooted cutting) it began up to 12 years of rigorous testing. It should be borne in mind that even *williamsii* hybrids take two years to flower from a cutting. Several cuttings then needed to be grown as stock plants from which cuttings are taken to propagate up to 100 or more before marketing. This in itself takes several years. But my father is a conscientious man and he was not willing simply to release unknown varieties on to the market, which is done all too often today. He grew each variety in his own garden in Cornwall to start with, then, if it was successful (had well displayed flowers, held up well and flowered freely in successive years, was self-grooming, had a good habit, good leaves, and did not show too much damage in the cold east winds in his garden), he sent it on to one or more of the International Camellia Society trial grounds in colder areas in the midlands and north of England, Northern Ireland and in Scotland. After all this, those that passed the test were duly launched in the nursery catalogue and with a bit of a flourish at one of the RHS shows in London. Les Jury's *C. x williamsii* varieties 'Anticipation', 'Debbie', 'Elegant Beauty', 'Elsie Jury', 'Joan Trehane' (named after my mother), 'Jury's Charity', 'Jury's Yellow' and 'Senorita' are all widely grown in all the camellia-growing countries of the world.

'Anticipation' and 'Elsie Jury' are two of the few varieties which are particularly successful in the hot, dry, climate of the Pretoria/Johannesburg area of South Africa as well as being favourites in the cold climate of Britain.

Professor E.G. Waterhouse of Sydney, Australia whose single plant of *C. saluenensis* was responsible for 22 seedlings from pollen transferred from nearby *C. japonica* varieties, from which we have *williamsii* 'Bowen Bryant', 'Charles Colbert', 'E.G. Waterhouse', 'Ellamine', 'Lady Gowrie', 'Lady's Maid' and 'Sayonara', all of which are still widely grown.

There is no doubt that the *williamsii* hybrids have had a tremendous effect and enabled gardeners in low light intensity, cold areas such as in the northern half of Britain to grow camellias successfully in their gardens when they would not have considered it before.

OTHER CAMELLIAS GROW IN POPULARITY

In addition to the tremendous impact which the discovery and distribution of the *williamsii* hybrids had in Britain and other areas of northern Europe other breeders, particularly in Australia, New Zealand and the USA, were hard at work creating new *C. japonica* cultivars and hybrids between *C. reticulata* and cultivars of other species. The search for 'something different' gets harder and harder, of course, but some outstanding varieties have been introduced since the 1950s. In the recent past the search has been on for miniature blooming camellia cultivars, those with scent, and, since the cold winters of the late 1970s in the USA and in Europe, for cold-hardy varieties. The elusive truly yellow garden varieties have also been sought.

In the USA the number of individuals who have had an influence on the camellia world is too many to mention, with enormous numbers of new varieties originated and registered since 1960. There are a few who have been responsible for a number of outstanding varieties which are now well established favourites throughout the world. Many of the newer *C. japonica* cultivars are also more floriferous than their older cousins, and the choice now available enables growers in the more extreme climates, whether hot or cold, to be more successful.

Dr W.E. Lammerts, an eminent scientist and camellia enthusiast, after much difficulty managed to make contact with the Kunming Institute of Botany and arranged for a consignment of camellia plants from its camellia collection to be flown to the USA in 1948. These were the first examples of *C. reticulata* cultivars to reach the West since the arrival of 'Pagoda' ('Robert Fortune' or 'Songzilin') in England in 1838. Many, unfortunately, were killed on arrival by the fumes from methyl bromide which was used by the plant health authorities to fumigate the plants. Another shipment arrived in 1950 and proved more successful. The naming of these plants caused subsequent chaos because western tongues had difficulties getting round their Chinese names, so they were given English names for simplicity. When communications with China improved later and more plants arrived in other countries it was found that there were some varieties masquerading under three different names! (They are listed on p. 38). The large, showy flowers of these marvellous varieties soon attracted attention and they formed the foundation for the breeding of many of the successful *reticulata* hybrids we grow so well today.

The Nuccio family nursery, founded in 1935 by Guilio Nuccio, has had, and still has, a huge influence on the camellia world. Brothers Joe and Julius, now virtually retired, their sons Julius (Juge) and Tom and others of the clan, have probably done more to enlarge the camellia horizon for us than anyone else. Their immaculate nursery at Altadena just outside Los Angeles has always had a large area set aside for seedlings under trial. These are mostly of their own breeding – they have introduced over 200 new varieties – but a number are from other breeders. From this area potentially interesting varieties are observed and, as they prove their worth, are selected and a handful are released each year.

The varieties cover the whole spectrum: *C. japonica*, *williamsii* hybrids, *reticulata* hybrids and other hybrids including those between a number of more recently discovered species. In addition to cultivars, their collection of over 40 camellia species is probably the largest available in the world and makes it a marvellous place to visit and to buy. Nuccio bred varieties widely available worldwide include the *C. japonica*: 'Bob Hope' (1972), Bob's Tinsie' (1962), 'Elegans Champagne' (1977), 'Fire Dance' (1957) but not registered until 1980, 'Grand Prix' (1968), 'Grand Slam' (1962), 'Guilio Nuccio' (1955), 'Maroon and Gold' (1960), 'Midnight' (1965), 'Midnight Serenade' (1973), 'Red Dandy' (1975), 'San Dimas' (1972), 'Scentsation' (1968), 'Silver Anniversary' (1960). Then there are the *C. japonica*s named with the family name as a prefix, 'Nuccio's Cameo', 'Nuccio's Gem', 'Nuccio's Jewel', 'Nuccio's Pearl'. Hybrids

'E. G. Waterhouse

'Dr Clifford Parks', a superb *reticulata* of great size and quality

include the x *williamsii* 'Garden Glory' (1974) which is so successful in cold climates, and *reticulata* hybrid 'Nuccio's Ruby' (1974). One of the most outstanding *C. vernalis* (*sasanqua*) varieties 'Yuletide' (1963) is also a Nuccio introduction.

More recent cultivars have been spreading across the world and appearing in lists of camellia show winners in the last few years: *C. japonica* 'Lemon Drop' (1981), 'Lipstick' (1981), 'Moonlight Bay' (1982). The work continues and each new catalogue is eagerly awaited by enthusiasts throughout the world.

Professor Clifford Parks, currently based at the University of North Carolina, has worked, both in his professional capacity and as a private individual, on breeding camellias including work on cold hardiness. C. x *reticulata* hybrid, 'Dr Clifford Parks' (1972), has been the top show winner in its section

A scene in the Descanso Gardens, California, where the plants imported by Dr Walter
Lammerts from Kunming, China, in 1948 may be seen

throughout the USA for many years. Dr Bill Ackerman from Maryland has also done much work on breeding for cold hardiness, with C. *oleifera* hybrid 'Snow Flurry' (1987) increasing in popularity, and for scented varieties like the delightful, miniature, scented C. *japonica* x C. *lutchuensis* hybrid 'Cinnamon Cindy' (1974).

In Australia the work of international registrar Tom Savige in producing his small leaved "Wirlinga Group" of cascading, small flowered hybrids is worth recognition, with 'Wirlinga Cascade' (1987) particularly outstanding. Edgar Sebire introduced a number of interesting hybrids, notably the C. *pitardii* 'Sprite' (1977) and the miniature C. *pitardii* x C. *fraterna* 'Snowdrop' (1979), which has been used extensively in further hybridisation work to produce more miniatures such as the popular 'Alpen Glo' (1985). Ray Garnett's work on scented hybrids includes the highly scented 'Sweet Emily Kate' (1987). Bob Cherry's Paradise group of C. *sasanqua* varieties has recently taken off in a big way, especially in Australia, with over 250,000 a year being distributed worldwide. They include some very small-leaved, extra compact varieties like 'Little Liane' and 'Paradise Petite' which have encouraged a surge in the popularity of camellias for topiary and small hedging as well as standards.

In New Zealand, Tom Durrant imported a number of what have become known as the Yunnan *reticulatas*, in 1964, and was also very active in encouraging others to enjoy their camellias, through his involvement with the New Zealand Camellia Society, which was formed after separation from the Australian and New Zealand Research Society in 1958. Tom's late wife, Bettie, was responsible for introducing one of the most successful hybrids

for small gardens in cold areas: the C. *pitardii* x C. *japonica* 'Nicky Crisp' (1979). She also added the C. *pitardii* varieties 'Persuasion', and 'Snippet' which are also good hardy varieties. Other New Zealanders who have had an influence on camellia introductions are the well known nurseryman Neville Haydon, who introduced his dwarf 'baby' family, 'Baby Bear' (1976), 'Baby Brother' (1991) and 'Baby Willow' (1983), all of which are hybrids between C. *rosiflora* and C. *tsaii*. Only 'Baby Bear' remains in extensive cultivation. His waxy plum red C. *japonica* 'Takanini' (1989) has proved very useful too. The hybrid 'Fairy Wand' (1982) and the scented hybrid 'Sugar Dream' are two of many bred by Os Blumhardt. Jim Finlay has also introduced a large number of scented varieties. All his work is carried out in a relatively small garden so he has developed a strict monitoring process, with all seedling flowers being given a rating of 1-5 and any which fail to make the grade, however beautiful the flowers, being ruthlessly culled. His early introduction, the C. *japonica* x C. *lutchuensis* hybrid 'Scentuous' (1981), has been followed by others which are still not widely available but are worth watching out for.

2

Camellias In A Botanical Context

The name camellia was coined by the Swedish botanist Carolus Linnaeus.

It was Linnaeus who created order in the world of plant nomenclature by giving each plant two-word Latin names which could be universally understood, no matter what native language each scientist or gardener spoke, or more relevantly, wrote. He organised them into convenient groups, giving each a generic and a specific name, equivalent to a surname and given name in our society. His *Systema Naturalia, Regnum Vegetabile* of 1735 published the names *Thea* and *Camellia* and for a long time controversy raged over which should be the correct name. The name Thea was attributed to Engelbert Kaempfer, a surgeon with the Dutch East India Company, who was based in Japan between 1690 and 1692. He published an account of his travels in 1712 in which he also described what we now know as *Camellia japonica* and *Camellia sasanqua*, and included a very detailed description with excellent illustrations of the tea plant. Linnaeus rejected the Japanese name for the ornamental camellias Tsubakki because it had a very un-Latin ring to it, and substituted his own invention, Camellia, in honour of a respected botanist, the Moravian Jesuit missionary, Georg Joseph Kamel, who lived and worked in the Philippines and probably never saw a camellia in his life. He died in Manila a year before Linnaeus was born, although his name, thanks to Linnaeus, will live on for ever.

The separate binary names, *Thea sinensis* and *Camellia japonica* were published by Linnaeus in 1753, but were informally regarded by many as a single genus from about the middle of the 19th century, but it was not until 1935 that the two genera, *Thea* and *Camellia*, were formally united, with Camellia the chosen name for the genus. The tea plant joined the genus *Camellia* and was given the specific, or species name *sinensis* because of its probable origins in China.

J. Robert Sealy, working in the Botanic Gardens at Kew, London, carried out further work and the RHS published his *Revision of the Genus Camellia* in 1958. In this he divided the

One of the newly reported red camellias, *C. jinshajiangica* seen growing wild near Dukou, Sichuan, China

Camellias from Camellia Mountain, near Huili, Scihuan

genus into 12 sections and described 87 species. Since then many more species have been discovered, especially in China.

In 1981 Chang Hungta of Nanjing, China, published his *Genus Camellia*, in which he reclassified the genus, forming four sub-genera, with 20 sections. The English translation, updated with assistance from Dr Bruce Bartholomew of California, USA, was published in 1984, with 201 species included. 'Chang and Bartholomew' is now regarded as the modern

basis for study, together with Sealy as a reference. To help with assessment a herbarium collection of all known species is held at Kew, together with full botanical descriptions. It is here that the type specimens can be studied, used as a standard for comparison, and as an aid to assess any future new species.

Botanists have continued to add more species; by 1991 there were 267, and more are still being discovered, although there is a debate about whether they are actually separate species or forms which have gradually arisen as a result of variations in climate and soil conditions in the wild or simply as a result of genetic variation. For example, some of the new species named by Chang Huyama in 1993 such as 'C. Jingsha jianica' are thought by others to be different forms of C. *reticulata*, the only differences being in some cases very minor ones such as hairs present at the base of the stamens in one form and not in another.

Some species are tremendously variable in colour and flower shape. C. *saluenensis* and C. *pitardii* var *pitardii* seen on Camellia Mountain near Huili, Sichuan, were all single or semi-double in form, but showed a great range of pinks – from rose through mid-pink, to a very light, almost creamy colour – and there were even some lightly striped flowers. There were deep, almost funnel-shaped flowers, flat bowl-shaped, frilled edges and small, medium and large blooms. The texture, shape and arrangement of the petals was also very variable. All were found within a 300-square-metre area, making them highly desirable for future breeding programmes.

These simple flowers are not generally cultivated in China, but wealthy Chinese citizens have been cultivating camellias for 600 years or more. The temple gardens of Yunnan are also famous for the large blooms of named varieties of C. *reticulata*, a species native to the province. How did these large blooms, more complex than the normally smaller, single or semi-double flowers, arise originally, all those years ago? Modern-day plantsmen, such as Bob Cherry from Australia, who have travelled and observed these camellias and a great many other genera, both in the wild and under cultivation over more than 20 years, believe that they arose naturally as occasional seedlings showing genetic variation from the norm. Informal double (peony form)

flowers are still very occasionally found in wild colonies amongst the more simple flowers, so this seems a reasonable assumption. *Camellia reticulata* was widely grown in plantations or in a semi-wild condition for the production of oil from its seeds for cooking. The plants were therefore under regular observation, and it is logical to assume that, amongst the tens of thousands grown from seed there was genetic variation amongst them, including some more exotic forms, in addition to the usual singles and semi-doubles.

There is a very long tradition of gardening in China, particularly around the Buddhist communities and in the gardens of wealthy land owners where colour and beauty are highly valued, and it does not take much imagination to picture some observant individual selecting from these and propagating from them.

(More detail is included under C. *reticulata*, on page 38.)

Crossing such as this, within a species, produces intraspecific cultivars. The 11th-century *Cha Hua Pu* written by Chao Pi lists 72 varieties of what we now call the Yunnan reticulatas. They were treasured and used as valuable gifts with the varieties producing the most desirable flowers being selected for propagation and given evocative names such as Butterfly Wings, Purple Gown, and even Ape's Lips!

Camellia japonica occurs naturally over a large area of Southeast Asia and, as a result of the very wide range of habitats that it has become adapted to, there is even greater variation than with C. *reticulata*. This has been used to good effect by camellia breeders for hundreds of years, with about 50,000 named C. *japonica* cultivars now registered, many of them introduced since 1950.

Interspecific hybridisation occurs in the wild where two communities of different species intermingle, provided their genetic make up, or chromosome count, is compatible. This apparently occurs between C. *saluenensis* and C. *pitardii* var *pitardii* on Camellia Mountain, near Huili in Sichuan Province, where the bees have little distance to fly to carry pollen from one species to another. (Botanists are, however, divided in their opinions, with one faction declaring that C. *pitardii* var *pitardii* is just a form of C. *saluenensis*).

BOTANICAL DESCRIPTION

Knowledge of the botanical make-up of camellias can be useful, especially when reading some catalogues, or when registering new cultivars. Botanical terminology can be complex, so this section has been selected to include only those terms which are relevant to camellia cultivation, without, it is hoped, detracting from the accuracy needed for precision.

Hybridisers and those with a desire for deeper botanical knowledge will find Chang and Bartholomew's *Camellias* of great interest.

THE PLANT – GENERAL DESCRIPTION

Camellias are evergreen trees and shrubs ranging from one or two metres to 15. They are of tremendous diversity. In cultivation we can find camellias which may be compact and rounded, or compact and upright. Some, such as C. 'Spring Festival', are almost fastigiate in habit. Or they may be tall and spreading or low growing and spreading. Growth may be pendulous, giving a bush with a tiered appearance, or branches may be stiffly held giving a much more formal outline. Some species have fine twiggy growth (C. *lutchuensis*, C. *cuspidata*) while others have a

heavier appearance (many forms of C. *japonica*). Their cultivars and many of their hybrids inherit these characteristics.

There are successive growing periods separated by a resting period during which flower buds form either at the ends of one-year-old shoots, or in some species in the axils of the leaves of those shoots where vegetative buds are present. The flower buds are formed in the axils of the lowest scales of these buds and soon become dominant, hiding the smaller vegetative buds. Usually there is a single flower, but in some species, notably C. *sinensis*, there are as many as six or seven at each axil.

The bark of some species such as C. *yunnanensis* is a particularly attractive russet brown, while the young shoots of some species are glabrous, and others quite hairy.

Leaves

These are alternately arranged on the stems with petioles (leaf stalks), 1.5 to 3mm long, and they may be smooth or hairy like the young stems. Leaf shapes and sizes vary enormously. The biggest problem for those describing the leaves of a particular camellia is that leaf shape and size also varies greatly on an individual plant, with young leaves, or even some of the smaller old leaves, being quite different from the older, larger ones.

Leaf margins may also be very variable, with most species exhibiting teeth, and some having wavy outlines. Colour is normally deeper on the upper surface and ranges from very dark to pale green, with a few such as 'Golden Spangles' and 'Benten Kagura' being naturally variegated with a cream or yellow pigment. Veins may be prominent or obscure, raised or deeply impressed, and sometimes the surface between veins is raised in bumps. Leaf surfaces may be glossy, smooth or matt.

Flowers

Camellia flowers vary in size from 1cm in diameter to 15cm or more. All have flower stalks (pedicels), although these may not always be obvious. The flowers are supported by sepals, and sometimes bracteoles which may fall off at an early stage, or may persist as far as fruiting. Less often, bracteoles and sepals combine to form overlapping scales (perules), which can be persistent to the fruiting stage as in *C. granthamiana*.

Petals, which nature has designed in prominent colours to attract insects to the blooms for the purpose of pollination, are arranged around the stamen cluster (androecium) with the innermost four or five attached to it. Sometimes, in many peony and anemone-form flowers some of the stamens lose their reproductive function and become petaloid, and in some, such as the anemone form flowers ' Bokuhan', 'Bob's Tinsie' and the much larger 'Elegans', for example, this state has become so advanced that the stamens are completely obscured. In some varieties, such as 'Elegant Beauty', the flowers may be quite definite semi-doubles, with no sign of petaloids for part of the flowering season, but at other times have prominent petaloids, making the flowers positively peony form. In others, such as 'Joan Trehane', the flowers may be peony form in one garden and a formal or rose form double 50km away. It seems to depend on temperatures at the time of flower bud formation and development the previous summer.

Stamens consist of two parts: the pollen-bearing anthers, and the stalks which bear them known as filaments. The filaments are usually joined at the base and may be arranged in a variety of forms from tubular ('Francis Hanger')

Flower forms **top row l to r**: single = J.C. Williams, semi-double = 'Daintiness', anemone form = 'Sundae'
Bottom row: loose peony= 'Betty Sheffield Coral', full peony= 'Tiffany', formal double= 'Donnan's Dream'

Camellia fruit

1st row: *C. trichocarpa, C. octopetala, C. polydonta, C. chekiangoleosa*

2nd row: *C. yunnanensis, C. reticulata, C. pitardii* var *yunannica, C. saluenensis, C. granthamiana*

3rd row: *C. japonica, C. pitardii* var *pitardii, C. kissi, C. yuhsienensis, C. sasanqua, C. edithae*

4th row: *C. rosiflora, C. tsaii, C. grijsii, C. sinensis, C. lutchuensis, C. transnokoensis, C. trichoclada*

C. octopetala

to the characteristic spreading form of the Higo camellias of Japan. In the loose peony flowers they are scattered amongst the petals and petaloids. Pollen may be any shade of yellow, white, orange or pink. It may remain clear in colour ('Nicky Crisp' and most of the C. *pitardii* var *pitardii* blooms) or darken to brown or black as they age ('Jill Totty' and most of the *williamsii* hybrids). This darkening is frowned upon in New Zealand, but either disregarded or, as with 'Jill Totty', looked upon as an attractive feature in the UK.

The gynoecium, formed by the stigma, style and ovary, is the central part of the flower. The ovary is generally divided into three sections, sometimes five. Each section of the ovary has its own style, bearing a stigma, which, when ripe, becomes sticky and receptive to pollen. The styles may be united for all or part of their length.

Each compartment of the ovary may have three or four ovules, which, if fertilised by compatible pollen, become the seeds.

Flower forms

Climate can make quite a difference to flower forms. For example, some cultivars such as C. *japonica* 'Desire' and C .x *williamsii* 'Dream Boat' have formal imbricated flowers in cool climates. However, where it is warmer, as in most parts of New Zealand, Australia, or the southern States of the USA, or under glass in colder regions, they tend to have bud-centred or 'bull-nosed' blooms. 'Dream Boat' also has incurved petals in hot climates, but this does not occur in colder areas.

Some varieties such as C. x *williamsii* 'Joan Trehane' have peony form flowers in the warm climate of New Zealand, where it was bred and rejected, but excellent long-lasting, rose-form double blooms in the cooler climate of the UK

C. polyodonta

(where it was seen in the author's father's garden by its breeder, Les Jury, on a visit to Europe and promptly named after her mother).

Also, many varieties have much larger flowers in warm climates, but produce small, insignificant blooms in colder areas. Some, like 'Anticipation', may have small, poorly formed flowers early in a cold season, but the expected large, beautiful, peony form flowers later on. Many of the beautiful Italian bred 19th-century varieties imported into the UK in the 1960s proved disappointing when grown outdoors in Britain, but came up to expectations in British conservatories. This response to temperature can

C. japonica

be quite critical and a disappointing bloomer can sometimes be turned into a success by a move into more clement conditions even within an individual garden.

Late blooming varieties like 'Joan Trehane' and 'Hawaii' often fail to open their flower buds in hot climates as temperatures are too high by this time.

When flowers are spent they may remain on the bush and need to be physically removed in order to keep it looking attractive ('Cecile Brunazzi' and many of the older peony or formal double *C. japonica* varieties). Others, like 'Charles Colbert', have flowers which shatter when over, while many, including most of the *williamsii* varieties like 'Debbie' and 'Anticipation' and the majority of modern varieties of *C. japonica*, drop their flowers as complete blooms before they go brown and unsightly. *C. sasanqua* flowers drop their petals first, leaving the central androecium and gynoecium, including the nectary which is found

at the base of the flower, for a few more days. In the UK this attracts late flying bees and wasps.

Flower size classification

Camellia cultivars have now been classified according to their dimensions, mainly to assist those trying to decide in which class to enter their blooms when staging their exhibits at camellia shows, but it can also be helpful when interpreting catalogues and buying plants at specialist nurseries.

The A-Z of varieties shows the six basic flower forms: single, semi-double, anemone, peony, rose form double and formal double.

There are further divisions according to the more detailed shape of the flower or the arrangement of the petals and of the stamens.

Flower colour

Camellia flower colours may vary greatly according to the local climate, soil and season, so it is difficult to be specific when describing even the flowers of an individual plant. Colours tend to deepen as the flowers age, and in hot weather or when the fertilizer application contains a high percentage of potassium. For registration purposes the colour description given in the first published description is the one used as the type reference. The RHS colour code is used to give as accurate a description as possible.

Fruit

In those countries where temperatures are high enough during the flowering season for fertilisation to take place and for the resultant fruit to develop, the study of camellia fruit can be a fascinating subject. The fruit of each species has its own characteristics and size variation is enormous, from the minute, 5-6mm C. *amplexifolia*, to the 10cm diameter of C. *crapnelliana*, or the even more enormous 12cm of C. *magnocarpa*, (*M. semiserrata* var *magnocarpa*). Their texture and colour when ripe varies from the brown, almost warty, woody

The striped fruit of *C.j.* 'Extravaganza' can be very ornamental

C. x *reticulata* 'Cornelian'

Pale pink forms of *C. reticulata* are found in the *Pinus yunnanensis* scrublands near the Yunnan/Sichuan border in Southern China

texture of *C. octopetala*, through the glowing russet woodiness of *C. crapnelliana*, to the green fleshiness of *C. japonica* or *C. tsaii*. *C. trichocarpa* and *C. yunnanensis* both have fruit with a reddish tinge, while some striped cultivars such as *C. japonica* 'Extravaganza' have green capsules with reddish striping. Each capsule has the same number of compartments, or loculi, as the ovary from which it developed, usually three, and each loculus contains one or two seeds. These are rounded, or rounded on the back and wedge-shaped on the front. Many contain a high oil content. When ripe in autumn, the fruit capsules split from the top and the seeds are dispersed, usually leaving the split capsule on the bush.

Camellias are native to South East Asia, with the majority of species found in southern China.

Most wild camellias are found in lightly wooded situations, on soil which is on the acid side, on well drained hillsides or in sheltered gullies. Some tolerate extreme conditions of winter dryness and exposure (see p 47, *C.*

pitardii), while others need heavy shade and tropical conditions (*C. nitidissima* and other yellow species). The species which are most widely distributed, such as *C. japonica* and *C. oleifera*, also grow in the most varied conditions of soil and climate under cultivation.

DISTRIBUTION AND ECOLOGY OF CAMELLIA SPECIES

Out of the 270 plus species now recorded just three have so far given rise to a significant number of cultivars for garden use worldwide: *C. japonica, C. reticulata* and *C. sasanqua* (including *C. hiemalis*). Another six or seven have been increasingly used in hybridisation programmes, and five or six more are appreciated by camellia enthusiasts purely for their individual beauty or perfume. In addition, *C. sinensis is*, of course, of enormous economic importance to the tea industry, and *C. oleifera* and some other species are important as oil producers.

Camellia japonica is native to Japan and five

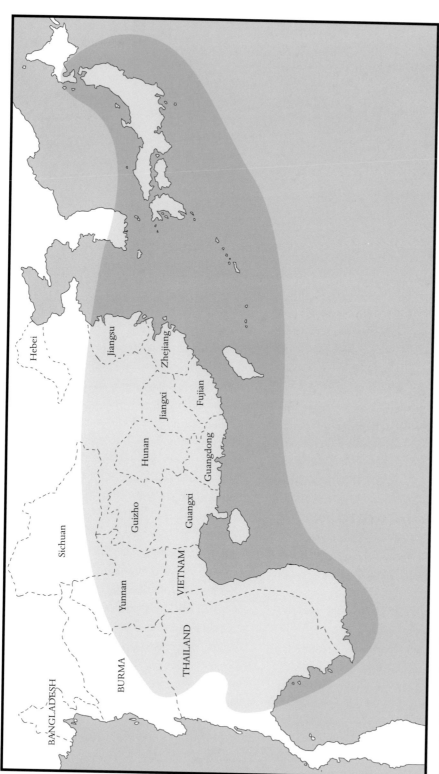

Geographic distribution of camellia species

The greatest concentration of camellia species is found in Yunnan and Guangxi provinces (70 in each), Guangdong (45+) Guizhou, Sichuan, Huan and Juangxi with 25+ each

Shaded area indicates geographic distribution of camellia species

The more usually accepted colour of C. *reticulata* is dark pink

provinces of China, and it is also found in Taiwan and Korea. Its climatic range is therefore from sub-tropical to the much colder climate of the north coast of Honshu island at latitude 40°N and this is probably one of the reasons why cultivars can succeed in a similar range of conditions in our gardens. *C. japonica* subspecies *japonica* var *japonica* has produced over 20,000 cultivars, by far the majority of all cultivated camellias so far introduced. *C. japonica rusticana* is used less frequently in cultivation; it is more well known as the snow camellia of Japan. A third subspecies, *C. japonica* subsp *japonica* var *macrocarpa*, is not grown as a garden plant but is sometimes collected by enthusiasts for its large red fruit.

The wild form of *C. japonica* var *japonica* is very variable, but is generally a shrub or small tree up to nine metres tall, with glossy green leaves which vary greatly in size, shape and colour. It has simple, single, five or six-petalled flowers which are typically of various shades of red, but pink and white are occasionally found. The stamens are united to form a white fleshy tube from the base to half way or two-thirds of the way up the length of the filaments, with yellow anthers at the top. The fruit is two to 3.5cm long and a little less across, with thick walls which become woody as they age, splitting to reveal three locules which each release one or two seeds.

The '*rusticana*' or 'snow camellias' differ slightly, usually having larger, thinner, paler leaves with hairy leaf stalks (petioles). The mid-rib and all the veins are conspicuously translucent. Flowers are more variable than the usual *japonicas* and may be various shades of red or even pink. The most important difference, however, is that these camellias spend their winters under deep snow, with the plants pressed close to the ground, so they have become adapted by having flexible branches, which spring up to flower when the snow melts. The lower branches become buried under leaf litter, and the colony spreads by layering. They have become so successful that they have been regarded as a nuisance by local people because they crowd out other plants in much the same way as a thicket of *Rhododendron ponticum* can dominate an English woodland.

'Purple Gown' is one of the 105 cultivars of *C. reticulata* which can be seen at the Kunming Institute of Botany

The *rusticana* camellias have not proved to have any particular merits in cultivation; they are not as cold-tolerant as might be expected because they have become adapted to the insulation of snow, but it is possible that some of the trailing or cascading varieties of *C. japonica* such as 'Taro'an' may well have descended from them and the greater variation in flower colour has probably been used by breeders in the past.

Higo camellias are a specialised form of *C. japonica* which have been selected over the centuries in the Higo district of Kumamoto Province on the island of Kyushu in southern Japan. They are thought to be the result of crossing selected plants of *C. japonica* var

japonica with selected *C. japonica* subsp. *rusticana* followed by repeated selection and recrossing over the years. They are mostly low growing and compact with the most robust, dark green leaves being particularly prized as they set off the beautiful, distinctive flowers to perfection. Higos have single or semi-double flowers, which may be irregular, bowl-shaped, flat, or even reflexed and frilly, with five to ten petals which are often thick textured and waxy, and occasionally phosphorescent. Colours are always clear and are often a very bright, white, pink or red, with many being bi-colours exhibited as bright flecks or stripes on a plain background. Their main glory is the very prominent collection of stamens, most often arranged in a flat broad mass, but sometimes in a dense upright column. There may be 200 or more stamens with petaloids sometimes intermingled, and they may be white, gold, pale yellow, or occasionally pink. In the centre is a prominent pistil.

Some Higos tend to sport very freely, with bi-colours frequently reverting to plain colours. They prefer warm climates similar to that of their base in southern Japan, to encourage flower bud formation, but they can be grown with success as far north as the southern half of England and in sheltered gardens elsewhere. They are occasionally scented and are also much prized for bonsai.

In cultivation there are *C. japonica* varieties to suit all areas where camellias can be grown, but it is important to select those which succeed in each region, or to find the right micro-climate in a particular garden. To compare the two extremes: those varieties which thrive in full sun in the 40°C of a Western Australian summer will probably fail to form flower buds in full sun in the cooler, duller climate of northern England. Conversely, those which succeed in the latter climate may well suffer from scorched leaves and failure of buds to open properly in the hotter climate, even under shade. The choice of cultivars for warm climates is certainly greater than that for cold areas where many people get vigorous growth but poor flowers or none at all on so many varieties, which will often succeed just 100 miles further south.

Professor Clifford Parks has selected a number of old cultivars of proven reliability and performance in cold climate areas, including parts of northern England and is using these to cross with selected, wild collected *C. japonica* from the cold climate parts of Korea near latitude 38°, which have shown little sign of damage at -23°C in the USA; the aim being to increase the range of free flowering, cold-hardy *C. japonica* cultivars for cold climate gardeners. (The results of these combinations could be even more interesting if they are then crossed with selected C. x *williamsii*, or with *C. pitardii* from higher altitudes in the wild.)

Meanwhile a number of modern *C. japonica* cultivars do flower more freely than many of those introduced before the 1970s. When selecting plants in bud, look for plants with a mass of flower buds rather than those with just a few; it does at least give an indication for future performance.

Camellia reticulata: This species is native to Yunnan Province in southern China and is the emblem of that province. However, it had been appreciated in the West as a semi-double or peony form for over a hundred years before it was realised that it grew wild in scrub and thickets and under pine trees at up to 9,000 feet in Yunnan. The type specimen for the name *C. reticulata* has a semi-double flower, while the truly wild form has single flowers with five or six (rarely seven) petals. For the botanical purists, the tag 'simplex' has been added to the latter, giving it the full botanical name of *Camellia reticulata* Lindley forma simplex Sealy.

C. reticulata grows as a loosely branched small tree or shrub up to 15 metres high. The leaves are often quite large: 7.5 to 11.5cm long and 2.5 to 5.6cm long, and are either broadly elliptic or occasionally elongated in shape. They appear rigid and leathery in texture and are dull green, sometimes matt, sometimes shiny on the surface. As the name implies, they have a network of clearly visible veins.

The flowers are single and most often rose in colour, although plants have been seen with both white and with pale pink flowers in the *Pinus yunnanensis* scrublands near the Yunnan/Sichuan border, and the beautiful Forrest-collected *C. reticulata* in the garden of the late Professor Waterhouse at Eryldene in Sydney, Australia, is a soft, two-tone pink. The filaments of the stamens are pale yellow or cream. The outer ones are united three-quarters of the way up from the base to form a fleshy cup or wide tube. The pollen is yellow. The fruit capsule is about 3.6cm high and 4.6cm across, light brown and rough in texture with one or two seeds in each of the three loculi.

Camellia reticulata has been cultivated for centuries both for the oil which is extracted from its seeds and for its ornamental value. Seventy-two cultivars are listed by Chao Pi in his *Cha Hua Pu* and there is evidence that they possibly go back to the seventh century. They were greatly appreciated during the Ming dynasty. More recently they went through a period of neglect and it was thought that many of the old cultivars were lost during the Cultural Revolution, but work done in the 1970s and 1980s by Xia Lisang and others at the Kunming Institute of Botany in Yunnan in finding and identifying many of the old varieties and adding a few particularly good wild clones has resulted in a collection of 105 cultivars, which can be seen in the Institute's grounds and in the gardens of the Golden Temple in the same area.

Many of the Kunming *reticulatas* are quite spectacular and have enormous, exotic blooms. Some are available from nurseries in other countries. They include the light red or deep pink 'Songzilin' which it is believed was brought to England by Robert Fortune in about 1838. It has several synonyms, including 'Pagoda' and 'Pine Cone' and about 48 petals in nine or ten whorls, giving the appearance of a pine cone opening its scales. 'Tali Queen' is enormous, having red flowers with about 30 petals in whorls, and a

The Golden Temple at Kunming shares credit for a well displayed collected of *C. reticulata* cultivars with the Institute

diameter which can reach about 22cm. Although virus variegated, the red and white flowers on the large plant of 'Damanao' or 'Cornelian' at the Kunming Institute are very striking and its non-variegated, red form 'Shizitou', or 'Lionhead' is seen in temple gardens all over Yunnan, especially in Kunming and in Dali – some are several hundred years old. One of the finest is on Zixi mountain, where there is a big tree, amongst which are branches of 'Tongzimian' or 'Baby Face', a small pale pink flowered *C. reticulata* variety. 'Captain Rawes', which was probably the first example of *C. reticulata* to be brought to England, in 1820, has not emerged in China, and plants have only relatively recently been returned to their native land! This beautiful rose red semi-double or loose peony flower can be seen at its best on what is probably one of the oldest surviving plants at Chatsworth House in Derbyshire, England.

Since 1949 many of these important camellias have been exported to experts in Australia, New Zealand, the UK and the USA, and there has been considerable activity amongst hybridists, with many excellent crosses made with *C. japonica*, *C. pitardii* var *yunnanica*, *C. saluenensis*, and even *C. sasanqua*. Most of those selected have large flowers and similar habit and leaves to the *reticulata* parent, and are therefore lumped together with them for most purposes. Some of those crossed with *C. saluenensis* or its hybrids have proved particularly successful as cold-hardy plants for northern European and British gardens and are treated for garden purposes as *williamsii* hybrids.

Winters in Yunnan tend to be dry and fairly mild, with cold spells including frost at night. Summers are relatively hot and wet. The soil is fairly poor and can have a high percentage of clay, but most of these camellias grow naturally on well drained slopes under light shade. Larger trees provide a mulch of organic matter from fallen leaves.

Most *C. reticulata* hybrids enjoy similar conditions, needing well drained sites and little if any shade, but they do need shelter from strong winds – hot or cold. They tend to be vigorous, open growers like their *reticulata* parents and should be given plenty of space.

The following *C. reticulata* hybrids should be treated like their *C. reticulata* parents: 'Buddha',

'Harold Paige', 'Lasca Beauty', 'Miss Tulare', 'Royalty', 'Valentine Day'. Others have smaller leaves with denser habits, and are cold-hardy for outdoor growing in the colder areas of Britain and most of northern Europe: 'Black Lace',' Dr Louis Pollizzi', 'Inspiration', 'Leonard Messel'. The last two are particularly tough and reliable in the colder areas.

'Francie L.' is one of the most versatile camellia cultivars to grow, with its large 'reticulata' flowers which are very freely produced even in moderately cold climates. In these areas its characteristic narrow leaves are, perhaps, too narrow and leathery for some peoples' taste, but it is certainly one of the best for training on walls of any aspect.

'Dream Girl', 'Flower Girl' and 'Show Girl', which have *C. reticulata* and *C. sasanqua* parentage have scented flowers in mid-winter or early spring, and are hardy enough to plant outdoors as five or six-year-olds in most of the colder areas, but suffer from bark split in cold winters if put out too young.

C. sasanqua: this species has been considered to be a geographical variant of *C. oleifera*, but is now firmly established as a separate species. Both have been widely grown for centuries in both China and Japan for the extraction of the oil from their seeds, although it is now recognised that *C. oleifera* is native to China while *C. sasanqua* is native to Japan. There are also physical differences, with *C. oleifera* having larger leaves and fruit. *C. hiemalis*, the 'cold camellia', and *C. vernalis*, the 'spring sasanqua', are often lumped together with *C. sasanqua* because they have similar characteristics, but are thought to be the result of natural hybridisation, probably with *C. japonica*.

C. sasanqua is found growing wild in groups as shrubs or as small trees up to five metres tall on the islands of southern Japan, particularly Kyushu, and on the Liu Kiu islands. It is found mostly near the coast, often on wide ledges on steep cliff faces, although it is also established at altitudes of up to 900 metres. It is therefore accustomed to exposed conditions from sea level upwards, although its association with other evergreens gives it some shelter. Soils are well drained and tend to be dry.

The foliage is dense and twiggy, with small leaves, mostly three or 4cm long, 1.5 to 2cm wide of a thin, leathery texture and glossy green. Leaf tips are sometimes long and pointed, sometimes fairly blunt, but leaf margins are usually prominently but finely toothed. The 5-7cm flowers, which are usually white, but occasionally pink or rose, are produced in autumn, carried at the tips of shoots and have six to eight notched petals which are usually unjoined right to the base. Petals fall after only three or four days. The flowers have a distinctive, somewhat pungent scent. The stamens are yellow with clear yellow pollen, forming a broad mass, from which the three arms of the central style, or the three separate styles emerge. The 1.5 to 1.8cm fruit capsule is rounded, and may be green with reddish shades, becoming woody and pale brown when ripe, splitting into three loculi, each of which releases one or two seeds.

C. sasanqua, despite its short-lived flower, has been cultivated in Japan for its ornamental value for as long as, and possibly longer than *C. japonica*. This is possibly because of the fact that a carpet of colourful blooms below camellia trees is considered every bit as beautiful and significant as the flowers on the tree itself.

C. sasanqua cultivars are most successful in areas with similar climates to their native islands. They do particularly well in Australia, the southern States of the USA and in the countries bordering the Mediterranean where summers are hot and winters relatively mild. They are also popular in the North Island of New Zealand. In Britain they tolerate the winter cold, but tend to get black speckling on the leaves in cold winters, sometimes followed by partial leaf drop, thought they recover with new growth in spring. The main problem is flower bud initiation following a late spring and a cool summer, so it is recommended that the warmest, sunniest place in the garden is found for them, ideally planting them against a wall for extra warmth. Alternatively they make excellent conservatory or cool glasshouse plants where the still air and additional warmth bring out the characteristic, slightly pungent scent.

In the south of England and in warm climate countries the more compact *sasanqua*s make good hedging plants, while others of a looser habit are ideal for training as fans or espaliers on walls or fences. Some are upright and make good columns, while others are rounded and formal and therefore more suited to growing in containers in a courtyard or on a terrace or patio.

Many of the newer cultivars, such as some of the Australian-bred Paradise group are extra compact and form dense bushes, suitable for low hedging or edging for a formal garden bed. They train well as standards or for topiary work. 'Paradise Little Liane' and 'Paradise Petite' are both good for this.

C. hiemalis is considered to be a *C. sasanqua* hybrid, the type specimen having semi-double, rose-coloured flowers 5-6cm across, but white flowers also exist. It is said to have been introduced to Japan from Shanghai as a pot plant for the Christmas and New Year trade. 'Shishigashira', the most widely grown *C. hiemalis*, exists in two forms. The slow, spreading form is one of the first to flower in autumn, with dark crimson red, small semi-double flowers, while the other is taller and later with larger pink flowers.

'Showa-no-sakae' has long been popular for its spreading habit, and is excellent for ground cover, with its fairly large, soft pink irregular peony form, long lasting flowers which do not fade even in full sun. It also has particularly good foliage. Its seedling 'Showa Supreme' is even better, with excellent foliage and a bigger, fluffier flower. 'Dazzler', although spreading, is more upright and open in habit, with particularly bright rose semi-double flowers in mid winter. It is ideal for espalier work.

C. vernalis is regarded by some as another *C. sasanqua* hybrid; this time with *C. japonica* being part of its make-up. The type specimen, collected in Japan in March 1896, has 6–7cm wide, white, semi-double flowers and larger leaves than the type specimen of *C. sasanqua*. They are spring instead of autumn flowering which has also caused some confusion, but many of its cultivars flower earlier, and are regarded as more cold-hardy than *C. sasanqua* cultivars.

Cultivars of *C. vernalis* are in short supply, probably because they have to compete with all the other spring flowering varieties of *C. japonica*, etc. but 'Star above Star' is noteworthy. Its flowers are white, shading to a soft pink at the petal tips, which are pointed. One ring of petals sits above the other to make a star shape. *C. sasanqua*, *C. hiemalis* (and *C. vernalis*) are usually treated as 'sasanquas' and lumped together in most nursery catalogues as such. They will all tolerate a more alkaline soil than most camellias, even slightly over pH7, needing less available nutrients. The majority enjoy full sun and are more resistant to root rot than most

species in hot humid climates.

Most species are native to areas in Southeast Asia where the climate is either sub tropical, or at least subject to only brief spells of frost, so the majority are not considered cold hardy, although several, used with *C. japonica*, produce some excellent cold-hardy hybrids. The following make reliable, interesting garden plants in warm climate areas or can be grown under glass in cold climates.

C. assimilis is from Hong Kong and the southern coastal areas of China. It is therefore suitable for warm climate cultivation or conservatories in cold climates. Grown for its lovely long, narrow red leaves and its mass of small white flowers, it forms a small, neat shrub up to about two metres. *C. caudata* is widely distributed in South China and in Assam, Bhutan, Burma, Taiwan and Vietnam. It has similar characteristics to *C. assimilis*, but the reddish colour does not extend beyond the young leaf stage. It forms a neat and attractive small tree.

Opposite: The leaves of camellia species vary greatly in colour, texture, size and shape
Opposite: The leaves of camellia species vary greatly in colour, texture, size and shape

1. *C. japonica*
2. *C. sasanqua*
3. *C. oleifera*
4. *C. nitidissima*
5. *C. yuhsienensis*
6. *C. grijsii*
7. *C. granthamiana*
8. *C. fraterna*
9. *C. kissii*
10. *C. transnokoensis*
11. *C. sinensis* 'Benibana-cha'
12. *C. sinensis* var *sinensis*
13. *C. saluenensis*
14. *C. rosiflora*
15. *C. tsaii*
16. *C. yunnanensis*
17. *C. cuspidata*
18. *C. lutchuenensis*
19. *C. transnokoensis* (young growth)

C. chrysantha. See *C. nitidissima*

C. crapnelliana: from the warmer areas of South China and from Hong Kong. It is therefore another species which is only suitable for gardens in warm climates. It has the most beautiful, glowing brown bark, 6-9cm white flowers, handsome leaves and very large – 10cm – fruit.

C. cuspidata is from a wide area of Southern China. It is of significance because of the hybrids produced from it, although it makes an attractive garden plant in its own right in warm climates, including Cornwall in England, with its long pointed leaves and masses of small white flowers in spring. These are 2–2.5cm across and have six to seven petals. In cooler areas the leaves tend to blacken from the tips in winter.

    C. cuspidata was fertilised with pollen from *C. saluenensis* to produce one of the most widely appreciated small-flowered hybrids 'Cornish Snow', which is successful from northern England to the warm climate of New South Wales, Australia. Its pink-tinged buds open to white, eight-petalled flowers, 5cm in diameter, which continue to cover the large, rounded bush from early to late. It has also inherited the tendency to reddish young growth. 'Cornish Snow' was bred by J.C. Williams (whose name is permanently recorded for the *williamsii* hybrids) and much appreciated by a Dorset nurseryman who was given a small bunch of it as a buttonhole for a social occasion, took it home and propagated it. 'Cornish Spring', a *C. japonica* x*C. cuspidata* cross, bred by Gillian Carlyon in Cornwall is also successful, with its upright habit and bright pink small 'cuspidata'-like flowers, although they need shade to avoid fading in bright sun. 'Spring Festival' is grown all over the world for its very narrow, almost fastigiate, habit and attractive 5-

6cm pink, rose-form double flowers. It too inherits the bronze young growth from its *C. cuspidata* parentage. Its other parent is unknown.

C. forrestii is mostly found in Yunnan in Southern China. A lovely graceful, small, narrow-leaved species with dainty scented white flowers, widely used as a container plant in New Zealand, and trains well as a standard, or for topiary.

C. fraterna from southern China, is a dainty species with 2.2–2.7cm, slightly fragrant, white flowers. It has a light and airy appearance, enhanced by the very fine hairiness of the under side of the grey green leaves and leaf stalks, and arching young stems, and of the bracteoles supporting the flowers. It produces its flowers in great profusion, often in clusters of two or three or more at the tips of the current year's growth or in the axils of the leaves along most of each long, young stem.

    Many of the most useful small flowered hybrids have been produced using *C. fraterna*.

C. granthamiana was originally found as a single tree in Hong Kong New Territories. It has pure white, eight-petalled flowers, 15cm in diameter, supported by very persistent grey brown perrules. The stamens are bright yellow, with golden yellow pollen. One of the beauties of *C. granthamiana* is its lovely large dark green leaves which have deeply impressed veins.

C. grijsii from southern China forms a compact shrub up to three metres, with small broad, prominently toothed leaves with obvious veins. The flowers are borne singly or in pairs, with five to six long white petals, and are sometimes scented but usually not. Two new forms, one pink, one double form, were seen by the author in

Kunming, China. *C. grijsii* has been regarded as synonymous with *C. yuhsienensis*.

C. lutchuensis hails from the Liu Kiu Islands. Its dainty small leaves which are a crimson red when young, and its masses of tiny scented flowers, make this species valued as a garden plant, or for growing in containers in the warmer areas of Australia and similar climates elsewhere, but too tender for cooler parts of the world. It is quite common growing wild in woodland in the Liu Kiu islands, and grows naturally to form shrubs or trees up to 20 metres high.

Its main value, apart from the above, is as a parent to produce scented hybrids, but its lack of cold-hardiness tends to be carried over to them to some extent, so many are best grown under glass in Britain and countries with a similar climate. One of the most well established is 'Fragrant Pink', a cross between the *C. japonica* var *rusticana* (Snow Camellia) cultivar 'Yoshida' and *C. lutchuensis*. 'Fragrant Pink' is grown in warm climates worldwide and is also more cold hardy than most *C. lutchuensis* hybrids, performing best in warm sheltered gardens in southern Britain, or under glass further north. Its reddish/bronze young growth is an attractive feature inherited from *C. lutchuensis*. Growth is vigorous and spreading, with pale green 6cm x 4cm leaves. Flowers are peony form, bright pink and 5.5cm across, 3cm deep, well scented, and produced early in the spring. 'Spring Mist' is another scented *C. japonica* x*C. lutchuensis* hybrid, this time with dainty miniature soft pink semi-double flowers produced very freely over the early to mid-season with a spreading habit and mid-green rather matt leaves. 'Spring Mist' makes an excellent plant for a hanging basket, or for cascading over a wall. 'Sweet Emily Kate' is a more recent scented hybrid, first flowered in 1983

in Australia. It is the result of crossing a *C. japonica* 'Tiffany', with a *C. japonica* x *C. lutchuensis* hybrid. 'Sweet Emily Kate' has flowers 7cm across, of peony form and of light pink, shading to pale pink in the centre. The slow growing, pendulous habit makes this an excellent variety for hanging baskets and for trailing over low walls in warm climate areas. 'Quintessence' is another *C. lutchuenesis* hybrid of similar habit and with particularly good perfume – it is available in most countries.

C. nitidissima exists in two forms, the most usual having the synonym *C. chrysantha*. Of the 21 yellow-flowered camellia species this is the one most well known outside China. It is native to the sub tropical climate of southern China's Guangxi Province, where it produces its lovely golden yellow, eight to ten-petalled, 2.5–4cm flowers in heavily shaded forests. It has attractive, deeply veined large leaves and grows vigorously under shade in gardens in the warmer parts of Australia, New Zealand and the USA and flowers well once mature enough. Under glass in Britain, it grows well but does not flower freely. It is valued more as a collector's item, but is being used by hybridisers to try to introduce yellow colouration into more hardy hybrids. Tens of thousands of seedlings have been produced, with no true yellow amongst them so far.

C. oleifera is found throughout southern China, growing as a shrub or small tree up to eight metres. It is a very widespread species, grown extensively in the past for its seeds from which camellia oil is extracted for cosmetic and culinary purposes. It is very variable, in habit, leaf and flower size, according to climate and soil. Its white flowers produced in mid-winter and early spring may be up to 9cm, with five to seven petals, with some forms scented. Growth tends to be vigorous and open, forming a small tree or shrub up to eight metres tall. The fruit are 3–4.5cm in diameter.

Some clones have also proved remarkably cold hardy. A specimen in the National Arboretum in Washington DC, USA was the only camellia in the collection there to survive one of the coldest winters in the 1970s and material from this plant has subsequently been used to form the basis of a hybridisation programme designed to produce more cold-hardy plants for cool climates. Dr Bill Ackerman noticed that C. sasanqua (or C. hiemalis) xC. oleifera hybrids using material from the Washington plant had better garden characteristics than C. oleifera alone and flowered better than C. sasanqua cultivars in cold climate areas. The aim has been to produce early, heavy blooming varieties of greater hardiness than at present available for autumn blooming, useful for the colder East Coast States of the USA, where they are designed to give good value before severe winter weather sets in. Most are similar to many C. sasanqua cultivars, both in their foliage and flower characteristics, and can be regarded for garden purposes as cold-hardy sasanquas. 'Snow Flurry', a white anemone form hybrid from this series, has a dense spreading habit and has done well in cold areas of the UK as well as in the USA, while others in the series are being assessed before release in Europe.

C. pitardii var pitardii and its relative C. pitardii var yunnanica are found in the wild in Yunnan and parts of Sichuan and other south China provinces, with great colour and size variation in the flowers (from rose to almost white). There is also great leaf variation, with many plants looking very similar to C. saluenensis, while others have a resemblance to the wild C.

reticulata. There continues to be confusion amongst botanists as to the clear identity of these three species. There is, however, a general acceptance that some hybridisation has taken place where they overlap in the wild, as in the area around Huili, Sichuan, where they are valued as flowers for the Chinese New Year celebrations. They are widely distributed in southern China in a variety of conditions from exposed sunny sites with little apparent organic matter for nourishment to quite shady sites under the canopy of other larger evergreens. Specimens of what the accompanying botanists identified as C. pitardii var yunnanica were found on an exposed mountain top in Sichuan at 3,000 metres in full flower in January, with 5cm of frost still in the soil at midday. The plants seemed to have adapted to high rainfall with their deeply keeled downward-pointing leaves, and were obviously adapted to cold, windy conditions.

pitardii var pitardii has already been used in a limited way by hybridists, the most notable result being the New Zealand bred 'Nicky Crisp' which was the result of a cross with C. japonica. 'Nicky Crisp' is now one of the most popular varieties in New Zealand, with its compact habit and dark green keeled leaves. It produces a profusion of pale pink semi-double flowers over the whole of the spring flowering season, which fall without discolouring. It appears to be very cold hardy. 'Snowdrop', a very useful C. pitardii xC. fraterna hybrid has lovely miniature single white flowers with pink tinges to the petals. This has produced the chance seedling, 'Adorable', a useful dense, upright grower with 8cm, formal, double, bright pink flowers. These two hybrids with C. fraterna are marginal as far as cold hardiness goes, but another, a chance C. pitardii var pitardii seedling, 'Sprite', with an upright habit

C. nitidissima (*C. chrysantha*) grows wild in the sub-tropical climate of Guangxi Province, southern China. It enjoys the humid conditions in the bamboo forests

and salmon pink, peony flowers although freely available in New Zealand, has yet to be tried in the UK and may prove more cold hardy. There is scope for much more hybridisation work with *C. pitardii* var *pitardii*, particularly with *C. japonica*, for production of cold-hardy hybrids.

C. rosiiflora from Sichuan and three other provinces in south China was, for many years, thought to be a cultivated hybrid, but it is now claimed to be growing wild in these four provinces and has been given species status. It is similar to *C. fraterna*, but has soft pink, six to eight-petalled flowers, 3.5cm x 2cm in dimensions. Its chief use has been to introduce

the small flowers and free-flowering characteristics it exhibits to a variety of hybrids. Nevil Haydon's 'Baby Bear' is a *C. rosiiflora* x *C. tsaii* hybrid from New Zealand, which is very dense and dwarf in habit; ideal ground cover for warm climates, and with its pale pink flowers in spring it also makes a good bonsaii variety.

C. saluenensis is found mostly in Yunnan province, but also in adjacent areas of Sichuan, China, growing in a wide variety of situations from stony, rocky, poor hillsides, to thickets in shady gullies. The author noticed that where *C. pitardii* var *pitardii* was found on the same hillside *C. saluenensis* was always in the more sheltered gullies lower down than *C. pitardii*. It has the ability to flower very freely in extremely shady situations in its native country, but because of its origins in warm, temperate conditions it is not exceptionally hardy. George Forrest, sponsored by wealthy English gardening enthusiasts, collected material from a number of different forms in different locations in China during the period 1913–1925 and these were distributed to the sponsors and others, including J.C. Williams, Colonel Stephenson Clarke, of Borde Hill Gardens in Surrey and Lionel de Rothschild of Exbury in Hampshire. In all cases it was found to flower freely from a very young age and to set seed very readily in these gardens in southern England. All shades of pink from rich rose through to almost white appeared, with sizes ranging from 3–5cm in diameter and six to seven petals. Some, such as 'the Exbury Form' are scented. Flowering time varies from late autumn to early spring. In addition to the great variability of flowers there is variation in the leaf size and shape, from 2.5cm to 5cm long and from 1cm to 2.3cm wide. The leaves are often crowded on the shoots and venation is obviously reticulate. The size of the shrub varies greatly too, from one to five metres. In all cases, both in cultivation and in the wild, the soil and climatic conditions must be a major cause of variation.

Although the single flowers are attractive in their own right *C. saluenensis* is most valued for its use as one of the parents forming the original *williamsii* hybrids because it conveys its free flowering ability in low light intensity situations to its progeny.

C. sinensis is the species from which most of the tea we drink is derived. The small-leaved form *C. sinensis* L. var *sinensis* has largely been supplanted by its larger-leaved relative, *C. sinensis* var *assamica* in most commercial plantations, especially in India, Sri Lanka and Kenya. The subject of tea is not relevant to this book, but many gardeners like to have a plant or two, and some grow their plants in the flat-topped, traditional manner and pluck the young shoots and leaves to make their own green tea. *C. sinensis* grows outdoors in sheltered garden situations in southern England, and in similar climates, or warmer, elsewhere, particularly

C. saluenensis flowers very freely even in the most shady situations

where there is good drainage and air circulation to imitate the dry but often quite cold winters it would get in China where it originated. (Its US Department of Agriculture [USDA] hardiness rating is zones 6-8.) Under glass it tends to get browning of leaf tips and some leaf fall in winter, particularly if the atmosphere is cold but moist, but soon recovers in spring with a new crop of leaves. There are many clones of both *C. sinensis* var *sinensis* and var *assamica*, with great variation in leaf size, shape and serrations, and in habit. Left to its own devices in its native habitat, it grows into a small tree or shrub, 1.5 to nine metres tall. The leaves of var *sinensis* are 4cm to 14.4cm in length and 1.5cm to 5cm wide, with larger leaves in the wild than under cold climate cultivation. *C. sinensis* var *assamica* is larger in every way, growing to a tree up to 17m tall, with thinner textured leaves, 7cm to 22cm long and 3cm to 7.7cm wide. The flowers of both forms have strong, curving pedicels, which hold the flowers clear of each other. The flowers are cup shaped, often in clusters of up to seven, with seven to eight white petals, and drop whole when spent.

The Red Tea plant, *C. sinensis* 'Benibana-cha', from Japan is attractive because it not only has small reddish pink, nodding flowers, but longish oval 4cm x 2cm red-tinged leaves and forms a dense, compact bush. All the tea plants flower early, in Australia before the *sasanquas* under glass in Britain at the same time as the later *sasanquas*.

C. transnokoensis is increasing in importance as a garden plant for warm climates (it comes from Taiwan), or container plant under glass, as its qualities become more well known. With its slow growth, slender branches, tiny leaves, which have a reddish appearance when young, and its clusters of beautiful little cylindrical white flowers, it really does give good value in spring, both when covered with its masses of white flowers, and afterwards when its red young growth appears. It is not unlike *C. lutchuensis* in general appearance, and its flowers also have a pleasant perfume.

There are variegated forms of this species, due to virus infection, but virus free forms can be found.

C. tsaii from Yunnan and Hunan provinces of China, has been in cultivation for many years, and there are now many clones of it, some from seed collected fairly recently in the wild. Its habit is so graceful, with its downward pointing, long, wavy margined leaves with their light green shiny surfaces (5cm -9.5cm long x 1.3cm to 2.9cm wide). *C. tsaii* forms a small tree 3-10m tall, and graces many Australian and New Zealand gardens, as well as a few in Cornwall and other warm parts of southern England. The flowers are white, and in some clones, occasionally flushed pink on some of the outer petals, the blooms are five-petalled and 1.6cm-1.8cm across, produced in mid-spring.

C. tsaii has been used for hybridisation, notably to produce 'Baby Bear'.

C. yuhsienensis from Hunan, China, has been claimed to be another form of *C. grijsii*, but everything about it is bigger, and the clones seen by the author do not have the same appearance, particularly of leaves, which characterises the clones of *C. grijsii* seen. The leaves are markedly downward pointing, 6–9cm long and 3–4cm wide, pale green and dull in colour. The glory of *C. yuhsienensis* is the strong, sweet scent of the often dense clusters of white flowers. These are 5–7cm across with five to seven petals clearly separated from each other. Apart from the pleasure given by the scent, either in a warm climate garden, or under glass elsewhere, this

C. yunnanensis 'yunnanica' is found all over Yunnan and has lovely white flowers with attractive stamens

species may have potential for breeding with other species to introduce perfume to the resultant hybrids.

C. yunnanensis: is found all over Yunnan and in parts of Sichuan, China, growing as an open small tree or shrub, 1.3 to seven metres tall, on open hillsides, by the roadside, or in thickets with other shrubs. There is considerable variation in leaf and flower size and shape, with leaves being fairly large, 3.7cm up to 8cm long, and 1.6cm to 3.5cm wide. Flowers are produced singly at the ends of shoots and are 2.5cm to 5cm across, white petalled with eight to 12 petals. Stamens are an attractive feature, with golden yellow pollen.

There are many more camellia species, mostly from China, which are gradually becoming available, some of which will make interesting garden plants for warm climate gardens in the future. Local specialist nurseries may have information on them as they become available. Different clones of the various species can be interesting to a collector too, with differences in flower size and even flowering time, as well as in habit. Sports, which differ significantly from the accepted descriptions, also occur; for example there are both double and pink forms of *C. grijsii*, and *C. oleifera* 'Jaune' is an anemone centred form of the species which has a mass of yellow petaloids surrounded by six white petals.

One of the best things about *Camellia japonica* cultivars is the glossy leaf texture
1. 'Grand Slam' 2. 'Margaret Davis' 3. 'Janet Waterhouse' 4. 'Elegans
Champagne' 5. 'Hagaromo' 6. 'Matterhorn' 7. 'Lovelight' 8. 'Holly Bright' 9.
'Konron Koku' 10. 'Midnight Serenade'

3

Cultivation

The species from which our garden camellias are derived come from a wide range of climates and conditions between latitudes 20 and 40° south of the equator. The descriptions of individual species (p **) give more detail and this, together with a bit of local detective work, should provide a clear picture of the needs of camellia cultivars derived from those species (and their hybrids) in each owner's garden. Lists of cultivars, with hardiness ratings are also given.

GENERAL SCENARIO – WHAT CAN BE LEARNED FROM WILD CAMELLIAS

A look at camellias growing in their natural habitats reveals that most are found in or on the fringes of lightly wooded areas. This indicates that most camellias appreciate some **shelter and shade**.

The sites are often on sloping hillsides with good air circulation.

Camellias like a **well drained soil**. In frosty weather the cold air will also drain to the bottom of hillsides. In hot, humid, summer conditions **good air circulation** reduces the risk of fungal infection, which is especially important in hot, humid conditions.

The tree canopy above provides fallen leaves which, after rotting, provide nutrients. Humic acid is a by-product of the rotting process.

Organic matter, once rotted, supplies nourishment and helps to keep the soil acidic. The climate in areas where most species relevant to our gardens originate is cool and dry in winter and warm and wet in summer. The camellias therefore have plenty of water to activate the bacteria responsible for the rotting of leaf litter and its conversion to minerals for use by plants in the warm summer months. Water also dissolves (if necessary) and transports minerals from the soil up into the plants when they need them – in their growing season. They have relatively dry roots in their inactive, winter period.

Camellias appreciate a **plentiful supply of water in summer** and early autumn, which enables them to take up any fertilizer which may be applied to the soil and to use it when they need it – for growth and flower bud formation. In winter, when they do not need so much water, and certainly no feed, they should be kept on the dry side, although **complete dehydration should be avoided,** especially in containers.

Frost, although occurring in many areas where camellias originate, does not 'set in' in these areas to any great depth in the soil. The days are warm and sunny enough to thaw most of it, which avoids root death from freezing and dehydration.

If growing camellias in cold climate areas it is necessary to prevent the roots from freezing in winter.

THE CHANGING SEASONS

An understanding of the annual cycle of activities in the life of a camellia helps in understanding its needs in cultivation.

Healthy camellias, like other plants, have a fairly predictable cycle, governed by internal plant hormones which are activated by conditions around them, notably temperature, light intensity and day length. The availability of water and soluble minerals in the soil is also important. The annual cycle of activity can be summed up as follows:

1   vegetative growth
2   flower bud and secondary growth bud
    initiation and development
3   flowering
4   fruit and seed formation and development.

Camellias have periods of rest between periods of activity. Autumn bloomers have little pause between bud development and blooming. Winter

and early spring flowering varieties in areas such as the southern States of the USA and Queensland and other northern Australian areas also get little rest in this period. However, spring flowering camellias in climates where significant frost is experienced have several months in winter when they are almost totally dormant.

There is another period when some varieties have a brief rest, following flowering and before growth starts. In other varieties growth starts before flowering finishes.

1   In order to provide a structure for flowering there must first be healthy growth.

    This actually begins with the activation of growth hormones in the root system below ground, so root growth starts first. This is to cater for the increased need for both water and minerals. Growth hormones are activated by warmth, and to a certain extent by light and by day length. The vegetative growth buds start to swell and finally burst into leaf. The plant surges into maximum activity.

    The first flush of growth lasts for about six weeks, then there is an apparent pause, followed by a second flush. In the coldest climates this does not always happen, and in the hottest there may be a third flush, or more on some varieties.

2   Flower buds start to form unseen in the longest, warmest days of summer, with large numbers of flower buds being formed when days are at least 13.5 hours long. For most camellias, particularly many C. *japonica* varieties, temperatures of 20°C or more are needed over a period of several weeks (not necessarily consecutively) to work, with the best results following summers with temperatures regularly over 25°C. Flower buds are formed on the current year's growth,

sometimes at the tips of shoots, sometimes in the axils of leaves further down the stem, or a combination of the two. The varieties which have the longest flowering season initiate flower buds on both the early and the later growth, provided the growing season is long enough to ripen the 'wood' sufficiently.

The time between visible flower bud formation and flowering varies enormously. One might expect the varieties which show evidence of flower buds first would be the first to flower. Not so! The autumn flowering *sasanqua*s are often the last to show their flower buds, at least in the UK, but the first to flower, just six weeks or so after their flower buds become visible. Spring flowering camellias carry their buds through the winter and some may not start to swell and to flower until six or eight months after initiation.

The period between the start of bud initiation (mid-summer) and winter is a critical time as the delicate, microscopic cells which form the building blocks of the buds and flower stalks all require a constant flow of sugars from the leaves, and minerals and water from the roots, with the whole transport system totally dependent on water. This is a time when a break in the water supply can be damaging. It is one of the major causes of poorly formed flowers or excessive bud drop before flowering. Both become apparent when it is too late to do anything except to prevent it happening in future.

During the winter, particularly in cold climates, camellias rest, ceasing all but the most essential activity. Food, in the form of insoluble carbohydrates, is stored in the tissues and converted into sugars by enzymes as required. Most is needed for the flowering period. Water uptake is minimal, and mineral uptake virtually non-existent during the shortest, coolest days of the year. Cool weather is thought to be desirable in winter to get good quality blooms in spring. It is said that temperatures below 10°C are required for several weeks, but current research is yet to confirm this. What is certain is that a combination of short days and high temperatures can lead to both flower bud and leaf drop. Perhaps this explains why our forbears lost so many camellias in their overheated 'stove' houses, and why they do not survive as houseplants in our centrally heated homes today.

3 This is the period which we as camellia enthusiasts value most. We build all our hopes and look forward to it with eager anticipation. For the plants it is, however, only a dress rehearsal for the more important ensuing stage.

When flowering takes place, whether in autumn or spring, the plant uses a great deal of energy, particularly if there are a lot of flowers. With high temperature, long summer days the blooms which result are large and demanding, with well spaced petals, giving a very full bloom. Flowers which follow cooler summer conditions tend to be smaller, with petals more closely arranged. Many varieties bred in areas which regularly experience hot summers are disappointing when grown out of their natural environment. Some fail to flower or produce blooms from which the centres fall out in a day or so. Others are disappointingly small. Conversely, there are varieties which are bred for cool climates and are quite different and often disappointing in hot regions.

4 The purpose of flowering, apart from giving us pleasure, is to attract insects to pollinate the blooms, to allow the camellia to

reproduce by forming seeds within fruit. These develop during the summer, ripening in autumn.

PRACTICAL CONSIDERATIONS

Four factors need consideration before plunging into a major camellia planting scheme: soil, site, climate, suitable varieties.

Soil

Soil provides not only a medium for anchorage to hold a camellia in place, but a medium through which roots can penetrate to gather both water and nutrients. Soil texture is therefore important. A dense clay soil with its closely packed, tiny particles provides a major obstacle course for the mainly fibrous root system of a camellia. It also holds water in wet weather so it tends to be more waterlogged and relatively airless in these conditions. Roots drown because of a lack of oxygen, especially at the lower levels where water stays longest. Root systems therefore tend to be shallow and under developed in clay soils, especially if rainfall is high and drainage is poor in winter. Growth and flowering are poor as is anchorage. Clay soils can be improved with the addition of plenty of leaf mould, well rotted farmyard manure, rotted bark or peat, to give organic matter. Grit or sharp sand improves texture and 'opens' the soil allowing better aeration, drainage and root penetration.

A light, sandy soil, with big soil particles provides the opposite conditions: easy for fibrous roots to penetrate, plenty of air for healthy root development, but rapid drainage which can be a handicap in dry summers where rainfall is low. This can be improved by adding plenty of organic matter as above. This will not only provide nutrients but help retain water, acting like a sponge.

The ideal is a free draining loam with an equal proportion of small (clay) and large (sand) particles, for root health and anchorage. Additional organic matter is needed to provide nutrients.

If the soil is prepared a month or two in advance it should be dark and crumbly in time for planting.

Soil acidity is also important. Camellias are only able to absorb the minerals they need if the soil is on the acid side of neutral (pH7): pH5.5 to pH6.8, although there are exceptions. Some C. sasanqua varieties are happy in slightly alkaline conditions, pH7 to pH7.5. Camellias in very acid conditions, pH4.5 or less, also suffer from chemical imbalance and fail to thrive.

Camellias enjoy a **free draining, acidic soil** with plenty of non-alkaline organic matter worked into it in advance of planting.

Site

When starting camellia growing in a garden this can be a chicken and egg situation because the choice of varieties is involved. Should the site be chosen first and the varieties selected to suit it, or should the varieties come first and a suitable site found for them? It is assumed that the basic suitability of the garden has been checked, either by using a pH testing kit or meter, or by observing camellias, rhododendrons, heathers or other ericaceous plants growing nearby, which indicate that the general area has non alkaline soil. The size, aspect and micro-climate of the garden all come into the decision making if camellias are to be more than the single impulse purchase of a plant which has to be 'fitted in somewhere'.

The first thing is to decide where camellias

Many wild camellia such as *C. pitardii* 'pitardii' and *C. saluenensis* grow amongst the pines

enhancement of home surroundings, to be carefully included in an integrated planting scheme, with due attention given to flower colour and form, time of blooming, leaf shape and colour, and the habit and ultimate size of bush required? If this is the case it pays to seek out the most sheltered corners with the kindest micro-climate for the pale-flowered varieties. It is sad to see what is known to be a beautiful camellia looking all scorched and battered by exposure to that unkindest combination of wind, unrelenting sun, and, in cold climates, frost as well.

A collector, or someone growing camellias for exhibition, may need to create the optimum environment to give his/her plants the best chance, putting up wind-breaks, providing irrigation pipes, shade houses and glass or polythene protection if necessary.

Some knowledge of the characteristic habits and requirements of individual varieties is a great help because there are camellias to fit almost any situation, which is marvellous as long as one knows which to put where.

Camellias flower over a long period, with some having a three, or even four-month flowering season. Their leaves, especially of *C. japonica* varieties, provide a lovely, glossy evergreen background to other plants for the rest of the year, provided they are given a chance to thrive. Varieties with large leaves, especially those held horizontally, or those with a thin texture, damage easily in exposed situations in either hot or cold climates, while those, like most of the *williamsii* varieties, or *pitardii* hybrids, with smaller, more leathery textured leaves are more weather-resistant.

Shelter from strong winds, and some shade, is beneficial, especially for *C. japonica* varieties. This may be provided by taller shrubs or trees, or by buildings.

are to fit into the future. Are they to be regarded as a hobby, to become a collection to be integrated into the garden scheme, but with landscaping and visual effect not top of the list?

Or should they be regarded as part of the

Climate

An appreciation of the general climate of the area and its suitability for camellia growing in the garden is, of course, a major consideration. It is assumed that the basic research on this has already been done. Those lucky enough to have conditions close to those in the wild, ie. cool, but not arctic conditions in winter, preferably on the dry side, and warm summers with adequate rainfall, are indeed lucky. Most of us are less fortunate, but still manage to grow and get immense pleasure from our camellias. Some have to adjust to climates which are colder than the ideal, while others have to cope with high summer temperatures, often combined with high humidity.

Growing camellias in cold climates

Many thousands of people grow and enjoy camellias in climates which are less than ideal for them, often because of long, cold winters, often with high rainfall, and because of short, cool summers. We have to take more care over the provision of sites for them, and to be selective over the choice of varieties. Fortunately, modern-day camellia breeders are well aware of our situation and there are now some excellent hybrids and C. *japonica* varieties which are more cold hardy than their forbears.

We also know more about micro-climates and appreciate that gardens in the same locality may experience very different conditions, depending on aspect and the shelter available. Different spots in the same garden even have different micro-climates, with a 'frost pocket down the bottom of the garden', or a 'hot spot just beyond the clothes line'.

There is a certain amount of confusion about what is meant by cold hardiness. There are two issues (1) survival of all parts of the plant at low temperatures, and (2) the ability to form flower buds and to bring them through the winter to flowering.

Survival

This, of course, means the avoidance of death, which, for a camellia, critically means the survival of at least some part of the root system and conducting vessels of the stems and at least some leaves. Freezing of the whole root system for more than a day or two is likely to kill the whole plant, as will the freezing of the contents of immature cells under the bark, which can occur especially in a 'soft grown' young camellia, which causes the bark to split vertically in strips all the way round the stem. The first sign of such damage comes later, when the camellia becomes, or tries to become, active in spring. It is then that the leaves take on a dull, droopy look and eventually fall – no water is reaching them from the dead roots or destroyed transport system.

This sort of total destruction is more common in container-grown camellias where no insulation has been provided around the pots, or in the garden when there is continual deep frost over a prolonged period and the ground becomes frozen to a considerable depth. If even just a few leaves survive at this stage there is hope, and container-grown camellias can be trimmed back and nursed back to health, with some overhead protection to keep the air still and shady, with light watering and no feeding until signs of recovery are obvious.

If, in mid-winter, it is obvious that root systems are frozen in their tubs, emergency measures can be tried, although it may well be too late. The main thing is to prevent further freezing around the roots, and to keep the air around the foliage as still as possible. A cool shed or garage is ideal as a temporary refuge until the freezing weather is over, with no heating except possibly very low background heating to keep the air only just above freezing. Gradual thawing is what is required. It is a mistake to try to thaw camellias artificially by taking them into a warm environment, or by pouring warm water onto the frozen soil. The sudden change will almost guarantee death.

Winter survival of container-grown camellias in cold climates is more likely if it is possible to prevent freezing of roots, by insulating the containers with bubble polythene, or plastic sacks lightly filled with leaves or straw, or by bringing them into frost-free areas for the winter or at least during extra cold spells.

Outdoor-grown camellias which appear dead in spring are best cut back severely, if necessary with a chain saw, to 10cm or so above ground

Most camellias are happy with the insulation which snow provides and have leaves which are designed to encourage snow and water to run off

level. Patience will be needed because it may be late summer before buds develop and burst into growth from the bare wood of the stumps. Many old European camellias were apparently dead after the bitter winter of 1987/88, when temperatures dropped to -27°C and below, and failed to rise above freezing for many weeks. Most of those which were cut back survived, and one land owner with an estate near Paris found that, after buying replacement camellias for his avenue of 'dead' camellias, he ended up with a double avenue as all the 'dead' ones recovered. It is wise to wait until camellia plants are well established, preferably in 25cm pots or larger, with strong root systems, before planting out in the garden in cold climate areas. This should be done in spring, after the weather warms up a little, to give the roots a chance to grow down below frost level before the next winter. Varieties which are known to be good survivors should be chosen.

On a less severe level, many people experience partial damage to plants in situations where, for example, the leaves on the top half, or the side of a bush exposed to the prevailing winter wind suffer damage or even loss in some winters, especially when sunshine is added to frozen leaves. The damage is due to de-hydration of the cells – lack of water in them due to the contents being frozen, and if then thawed, removed rapidly by evaporation by the wind, at a time when they are unable to draw more from the frozen or inactive roots. The remedy is to move the plants to a more sheltered site, or to provide a wind-break/shade structure or larger, less vulnerable tree/shrub to shield the camellias. Horticultural fleece draped over the bushes is excellent as a temporary insulator. If damage does occur any leafless branches should be cut back if they show no signs of growth by mid-summer.

The ability to flower in cold climate areas

Many *C. japonica* varieties are great survivors, withstanding some of the worst winters better than any others, growing well in summer, with glossy green leaves. But they may have no flowers, sometimes for year after average year, especially in the cooler climates of the northern parts of Britain, northern Europe, northern States of the USA, and in the southern half of the South Island of New Zealand. Investigations reveal that these plants are of varieties which have been bred and are highly successful in warmer climates, but are simply not suited to colder areas where summers are also often short. Most of them require a long growing season to allow enough time for them both to grow and become sufficiently mature to form flower buds. Others need longer periods of summer temperatures over 15°C (62°F) for flower bud formation, while still others form buds which fail to open properly or produce small, scruffy flowers because temperatures are too low for them at flowering time. Many camellias shed some of their flower buds during the winter as a means of thinning the future burden on the plant, but heavy bud drop is often the first sign of cold weather damage in winter, and, again, it is often the same varieties which suffer this way year after year. Hope springs eternal, but it is no good suffering this sort of disappointment every winter so these plants should either be dug up and moved to a more sheltered, warmer site or disposed of.

Once through the worst of the winter weather the flower buds start to swell and show colour. In some seasons when there is severe frost at flowering time, flowers will be browned and buds will also be damaged as they swell. The warmth of the sun can encourage rapid thawing

Many of the early flowering varieties bloom cheerfully under their blanket of snow

which increases the risk of such damage, so early flowering varieties are best planted where they will get some shelter, although there are almost certain to be periods during their flowering season when the weather is more congenial and flowers can be enjoyed.

Choice of variety is certainly important and even critical in the really cold areas such as in Germany and in northern Britain and the colder areas of the USA.

There are now many varieties which are rewarding and flower freely in these cold areas, notably the *williamsii* varieties, *pitardii* hybrids and some *C. japonicas*.

Growing camellias in hot climates

Those who have camellias in the warmer parts of the world have to contend with summer temperatures which rise to over 40°C in summer, with high light intensity. Some have a Mediterranean climate, with dry heat, others have more tropical high humidity. In all areas summer irrigation is essential, with good mulching to conserve moisture in summer and in hot, dry climates, overhead sprinklers cool plants down in severe heat. Shade, except for most *C. sasanqua* and some *C. reticulata* varieties is also needed, especially for *C. japonica* varieties. Most camellias thrive in shaded conditions in warm, humid summers, growing well and producing handsome blooms the following spring. The main problem is 'die back' (*Glomerella cingulata* or *Phomopsis sp*). It can be discouraged by encouraging good air circulation around and within the bushes by spacing them well apart at planting, and by, as the New Zealanders say 'pruning so that a bird can fly through the bush'. Diseased shoots, which tend to be the younger ones, should be cut out and burned. Fungicide sprays may also be used. *Glomerella* and other fungal diseases tend to be varietal in their preferences, being particularly severe on many hybrids with *C. saluenensis* in their breeding, which means that some *williamsii* hybrids are not always happy in hot, humid climates. Local advice on choice of varieties is helpful here.

Suitable varieties

The choice of varieties for the various conditions is important because we are dealing with what is a long-term investment; something which should give pleasure for the lifetime of the owners and beyond. The lists included in this book are essentially incomplete and designed to give guidance rather than provide hard and fast rules.

Specialist nurseries in the locality, or at least in the country concerned, camellia societies, and a talk with exhibitors at flower shows where camellias are exhibited should provide the most relevant and detailed information and help. Basically, the *williamsii* varieties are particularly recommended for the cooler extremes of climate and the autumn flowering *C. sasanquas* for the hotter extremes. In between, a mix of *C. japonica*, *williamsii* and *C. reticulata* will be rewarding for spring flowering, with the *sasanquas* also doing well in areas where summer warmth is sufficient to encourage flower buds. Collectors will almost certainly wish to try some of the species, and may wish to select some particular group, such as the Higos, or maybe the miniatures, as a specialist interest. Others may wish to have a go at training camellias as standards, or as globes or peacocks, hanging baskets, fans, espaliers or even as bonsai. Camellia hedges, both low to replace Box (*Buxus sempervirens*), or higher to replace more traditional evergreens like laurel (*Prunus laurocerasus*), or privet (*Ligustrum vulgare*), are also increasingly grown. There are varieties for all these purposes.

Where conditions are particularly cold in winter, camellias give enormous pleasure when grown under glass, or at least kept under glass in the winter months. Scented varieties are highly valued for this purpose.

Colours, flower sizes and flower forms are personal choices, as are the expected ultimate height and growth habit of varieties. It is sensible to choose varieties which grow to the scale of the garden and the site within it. For instance, it is good policy to select low growing, spreading varieties to plant under windows, or towards the front of beds, while upright, vigorous camellias are best for backgrounds and to hide ugly features. Vigorous growers are hard work in small gardens because, although they can be controlled by regular pruning, slower growers are much more appropriate and easier to manage. Floppy habits are marvellous for espalier work; small-leaved camellias for hedging and topiary work; narrow growers fit into tight corners; wide ones fill large spaces, and so on.

It is easy to make an impulse purchase of an eye appealing, beautifully balanced, strictly tamed plant from a garden centre only to discover that the variety is naturally spreading and open. It is also unfortunate that many of the plants now being sold trained on wooden trellises are actually naturally compact and bushy, but did not make the grade for that purpose in the production nursery and sell better with branches pinned back on a framework.

GROWING CAMELLIAS IN THE GARDEN

Having decided that the proposed site is suitable for camellias, the ideal is to prepare it three or four months ahead of planting. This applies where camellias are integrated into the general garden scheme and to collections planted in the ground. A planting plan, with the chosen varieties marked on it with appropriate spacing worked out, is also an ideal and worth giving a good deal of thought to. It is frustrating to discover at a later date that vigorous, upright growers are obscuring those with an attractive, low, spreading habit which should have been planted in the front of the border.

Site preparation
Soil preparation starts with the removal of all weeds, especially persistent perennial weeds like couch grass and ground elder. Soil improvement

then follows, with virtually all soils benefiting from the incorporation of some form of organic matter, well mixed with the garden soil to at least a spade's depth, preferably more, to give a good environment into which the growing root system can advance. A surface area of around a square metre should be allowed for each plant for the same reason. Organic matter generally should not include chalk or lime, but spent mushroom compost (which does include it) has been used with no harmful effects when incorporated with very acid soil (pH4.5). More usual are very well rotted horse or cow manure (rotted to the stage where it crumbles in the hands), rotted leaf litter or peat.

Any additional soil improvements relevant to the particular soil type should of course be carried out at this stage. This applies especially to heavy soils with a high proportion of clay. These need to be broken up to create a crumbly texture, using a fine grit or sharp sand which should become well mixed and this really should be done three or four months ahead of planting.

As a rough guide, use one wheel-barrowful of peat or leaf mould per square metre, or half that amount if using manure. Where relevant, add just under one barrow of grit for a heavy clay soil, or half the quantity for a less dense one.

Planting
Most camellias are bought in plastic pots. They should be kept in a cool, sheltered, frost free place until their site is ready for them. Since there is little disturbance, and therefore little damage to roots, when transferring container grown camellias from their pots to their planting sites, planting may be done at any time of the year to suit the wishes and convenience of their owners. It is worth noting, however, that the root systems of container grown plants are restricted to the

size of their pots. Small plants, of 60cm or less, with small, shallow, root systems are more vulnerable to extremes of heat, drought and cold, than larger plants in larger pots, so autumn or winter planting is best for them in hot climates, and spring is preferable in cold areas. Larger plants with deeper root systems are less susceptible, but extra care should still be taken until they are well established, particularly to make sure that they, too, get enough water to prevent their root systems from drying out. This is particularly true of summer planted camellias in any climate.

When all is ready, the plants should be given a good soaking so that the whole root system is saturated and the pot can be more easily removed. The root system should be checked and should be well established, but not so 'pot bound' as to be densely matted with little soil visible. Occasionally a single tap root may be seen curling its way round the inside of the pot and it pays to cut it back sufficiently to prevent it forming a circle, otherwise root strangulation may result. This is when the root system fails to develop properly, being confined to the area around the encircling tap root instead of penetrating the ground sufficiently to provide anchorage, and to be able to draw upon water and minerals from a wide area. If the plant manages to grow upward it is likely to be blown over in a few years. It is more likely to fail to thrive and to end up on the bonfire. Matted fibrous roots may be gently teased to release them – taking care not to bruise them too much – or the most matted section removed with a sharp knife.

The camellia is then ready for planting, taking care to firm the soil round the roots so that the final level is no higher than it was in the pot from which the plant came. More young camellias die in their first year following planting as a result of being planted too deep, than from any other cause, as the result of bark at the base of the stem being more or less permanently moist. This results in rotting and consequent disruption to the conducting vessels just under the bark, which in turn results in water and minerals failing to reach the tops of the plants and sugars from the leaves reaching the roots. All camellias should be given a thorough watering, to the point where water saturates the ground, immediately after planting and then be left to settle.

Labelling

Labels supplied with the camellias are useful at the time of purchase and it is worth keeping a record of the variety either on a planting plan, or by re-labelling at planting. It is surprising how many visitors ask 'what variety is that?', and memory lets you down, or the label has faded beyond recognition. Plastic stab labels are useful as hanging labels, with holes punctured at the tip through which plastic-coated wire may be threaded. Genuinely weatherproof pens are hard to find, but good quality stationers worldwide stock the Edding 2000 which, although the point blunts quickly, is waterproof for at least five years. If the label is fastened with a wide loop around an inner, shaded branch it is safe for several years and is less likely to fade than when put in a more exposed place. It is wise, however, to check, and if necessary adjust the wire every year or so to prevent it cutting into the branch. For those who wish to formalise their labelling system, there are some very attractive permanent labels which can be bought from specialist label companies which exhibit at all the major flower shows.

Staking

The need for staking depends on both the size and shape of the camellias planted. The main reason for support is to prevent the plants rocking in the wind, which prevents roots from becoming established, so it stands to reason that tall plants which offer wind resistance will need staking in a windy spot while shorter ones of more compact habit will probably not need it. Stakes should be tall enough to give support for the next two years or so, by which time the roots should have become established and be doing their job as anchors. It is a good policy to avoid pushing stakes through the root system to avoid damage. Large plants, particularly those which have been dug up and moved and have large root systems, may need two stakes pushed into the soil, one on either side of the root ball, with a bar between them to which the camellia can be fastened. Broad plastic ties which do not cut into the stems are freely available at garden stores.

Mulching

A mulch is defined as 'a cover to protect roots of plants or to conserve moisture'. It can also help to stifle weeds. It has been recommended as an insulation against frost penetration, but research in the USA indicates that it also prevents daytime thawing and thus encourages deeper penetration of regular night time frost in prolonged spells. Mulch is actually removed in those areas for the winter months!

Mulches reduce evaporation from the soil so they are very important in all areas during summer, and in climates with warm dry winters they are beneficial all year round. Wood chips are the most common material to use, especially since home wood chipping machines are now so widely available and bags of bark mulch are sold in every garden store. Gardens where unrotted

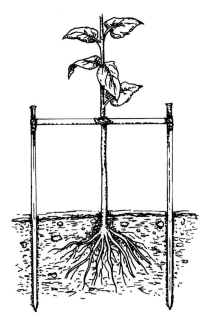

Staking a large camellia:
Staking on either side of the main root system is best for large camellias – fewer roots will be damaged

mulches are used will need to have an extra boost of high nitrogen fertilizer to cater for the needs of the bacteria responsible for the rotting process. Relatively little nourishment is available for camellias from these mulches, but they do shrink as they rot and will need topping up every two years or thereabouts.

Mulches should be applied to a depth of at least 75cm (three inches) and should not be in direct contact with camellia stems to avoid future stem rot.

Moving established camellias

Sometimes it is necessary or desirable to dig up and replant quite large camellias and this often gives cause for worry. It need not, as even large, 20-year-old plants can be moved. Obviously the larger the plant the greater the risk, and most suffer some form of setback, usually in yellowing of leaves and a failure to flower the following season, but the vast majority do recover.

They appreciate sites with good drainage, even surviving, but not thriving in near vertical shale slopes in the wild

In warm climates autumn or winter are good times to move plants, and in cold areas either autumn, while the ground is still warm and the roots active, or spring, just before growth starts. Site preparation should be done in the usual way so that all is ready for the move. Then, a sharp spade is used to dig round the outer limits of the root system, severing any roots cleanly and working down, underneath the plant with positive, sloping cuts. Some approximate idea of the limits of the root system can be given by looking at the size and shape of the bush. A tall, narrow camellia may well have a deep tap root, while a short, squat plant is likely to have a compact, shallowish root system.

Once the plant is free it should be lifted gently, taking care to keep the root ball as intact as possible. If necessary, a sheet of heavy-duty polythene is used to slide the plant onto and to carry it to its new site.

The root ball may be placed on a small mound in the centre of the planting hole especially if the soil is on the heavy side. Excavated soil, mixed with peat or leafmould etc is then shovelled in round the roots and the soil firmed down. A really thorough soaking is then given, until the site looks saturated. The addition of a stake, or stakes may be necessary if there is likely to be wind rocking, and a good layer of wood chips or other mulch added, followed by a slow acting granular fertilizer (if moving in spring) to finish off.

If the weather is hot or windy, or worse still, both, it pays to spray the foliage with cold water three or four times during the day for the first four or five days. This reduces water loss from the leaves (transpiration) during the critical period when the damaged roots are repairing themselves, and growing the all important root hairs through which virtually all their water is absorbed.

Watering

Having seen camellias growing and flowering, if not exactly thriving, in apparently dust dry, barren situations in the wilds of Sichuan, southern China, it rams home very forcefully the fact that camellias are incredibly tough, and resistant to drought, at least during the winter and early spring.

The time when they need water, and get it in the wild, is during the growing season, when they are at their most active, in late spring through summer and into the autumn. They need it, not just as an essential ingredient in its own right, but also as a means of transporting vital minerals up from the soil (and sugars, made in the leaves) to all parts of the plant. The minerals also have to be first dissolved in the water in the soil, of course. A vigorous, actively growing camellia, like C. x *williamsii* 'Debbie', will need more minerals and more water than a slow growing, compact one like C. *japonica* 'Hassaku'.

A well established camellia will have an enormous network of roots, with a huge surface area, sufficient to glean its mineral requirements from virtually any site and it is probably unnecessary to feed or water it at all. Small plants are not so lucky and need extra help, especially in sandy soils which drain extra rapidly and dry out quickly in a drought. Container-grown camellias, of course, need even more care because their roots are so restricted.

It is always good practice to collect rainwater from the house roof in a tank or water butt. This water is free, unpolluted with chlorine and slightly acidic. Most people, however, have to rely on the public water supply for their gardens, which is fine when it is a reliable one, with no drought restriction orders. If there is a need to water heavily over a prolonged period those with an alkaline supply and garden soil leaning towards the alkaline may have to use an acidifying chemical fertilizer instead of a more neutral one. Those with naturally acid soil need have no fears.

The most critical time when a good supply of water is essential is when the flower buds for the following season are forming. This is from mid-summer till early autumn, just when many people go away on holiday. If there is a break in the water supply to the areas where the flower buds are developing neither they nor their flower stalks will form properly. The cells in this area will be distorted and the weakness will become apparent at the first sign of stress in the following months. In cold climates a carpet of flower buds on the ground after the first significant frost is not uncommon and can usually be traced back to water deprivation during a dry spell in late summer, especially if flower bud drop does not occur here normally.

An overhead sprinkler system, or a hand held spray of water adds extra insurance as it creates the degree of humidity camellias would be enjoying if they were in the wild.

Above all, it is important to make sure that the added water reaches right down into the soil and is not just confined to the top few centimetres. It is far better to leave the hose or sprinkler on for a longer period once a week or so, depending on conditions, and then to turn it off until the soil really begins to dry out. This will encourage the plant to send its roots down deeper and makes sure the roots get enough each time. Watering little and often not only deprives the existing deeper roots of water, but discourages the root system from going down deeper into the soil where they would be less vulnerable in future dry seasons, and to frost damage in winter too. A root system restricted by lack of water is also one which may well lack the ability to take in enough minerals. How many of us have seen poor, starved, yellow plants in sandy soils?

It is wise to dig down near, but not amongst the roots, after watering every now and again to see how far the water has penetrated.

Soil fertility and feeding

The subject of which fertilizer to use causes much discussion. Most of us have our favourites, which become relied upon as a result of trial and error. It can, however, reduce the risk of error if we know more about dietary likes and dislikes of camellias. It may be that the decision is not to feed at all, or it may help to make a choice when faced with the huge choice of fertilizers now available. Most have an analysis of ingredients on the container giving the proportion of main elements and a list of minor elements.

In order to make the basic 'to feed or not to

feed' decision some knowledge of the mineral content of the soil or compost is useful, as well as an understanding of the usefulness of the ingredients in the fertilizers on offer. A good, fertile loam soil, with plenty of rotted organic matter in it, already has a reasonable supply of available minerals suitable for most plants. As has already been established, a mature camellia will need no extra feed in this type of soil.

Micro-organisms responsible for the rotting of organic matter are activated in the warm soil of summer, eventually setting free the minerals required by the plants at just the time they need them most – when they are in active growth. 'Eventually' is used because unrotted leaf mould, bark, wood chips, etc, need nitrogen themselves to carry out the rotting process. Hence the need to make sure added organic matter is either well rotted, or extra nitrogen is added for the purpose. Sandy soils lacking in organic matter are often nearly sterile and if they remain short of organic matter will probably need a regular boost in order to provide enough minerals for the needs of older plants as well as young ones.

Unimproved clay soils are often poor because although the necessary minerals may be present, they tend to be chemically unavailable to plants such as camellias.

It is the needs of young plants and plants in containers which are so dependent on added fertilizer. Mature plants, especially those in poor soils, may need initial booster feeding to correct deficiencies, by far the most common of which is nitrogen deficiency, followed by more balanced fertilizer applications from then on.

The vital elements

Nitrogen (N), phosphorus (P) and potassium (K) top the list in the amount required, but are not necessarily the most important minerals needed by camellias. They are regarded as the major elements, followed by calcium (Ca), iron (Fe), magnesium (Mg) and sulphur (S). In addition, there are the micro-nutrients: aluminium, boron, copper, manganese, molybdenum, zinc and others. All are needed for vital chemical processes within the body of the plants, even if only required in minute traces – 'trace elements'. Where deficiencies or excesses are not mentioned they are not considered to be significant problems in camellia culture. All excesses should be dealt with by flushing surplus minerals out of the soil with clean water as soon as symptoms are identified.

Nitrogen (N). This is taken up from organic matter in the soil in a suitably acceptable form, after a complicated series of chemical processes. Most of these involve soil fungi and bacteria, which work best in a healthy, well aerated soil with plenty of organic matter for them to work upon. They are at their most active in the top layers of the soil, which suits camellias well due to their high proportion of surface roots. They act by first digesting the organic matter (including granular organic fertilizers), using available nitrogen in the soil in the process. This builds up their own mass. When they die this sets free the nitrogen in a form suitable for roots to absorb. Soil bacteria therefore take before they give, hence the need for extra nitrogen to break down un-rotted leaf mould etc. and the time lapse between applying solid organic fertilizers and the appearance of any benefit.

Some organic fertilizers are relatively quick acting though, notably dried blood (15% N) and urea (46% N), which are capable of 'greening up' a nitrogen-deficient camellia in less than a week. Chemical fertilizers, or 'straights' are readily available and are quick acting. Ammonium nitrate (34% N), and particularly ammonium sulphate (21% N) also have an acidifying effect on the soil, and both are suitable for camellias, which, it has been shown, prefer their nitrogen in 'ammonium' form.

Nitrogen is the most quickly available, and also the most rapidly used, element. It is used for protein formation, for growth and for building up the body of the plants. Camellias carry a high proportion of body in the form of a mass of evergreen leaves and they have a peak demand when more are added in spring, hence the need for a 'high nitrogen' fertilizer at this time. Within the plant the use of nitrogen is tied up with the activity of the green chlorophyll in the leaves. Light is needed as the source of energy to drive this process.

Nitrogen deficiency symptoms: Pale leaves, yellow in severe cases. Poor growth, spindly, sickly-looking, stunted, plants which are more prone to damage in adverse weather conditions. Growth is also delayed in comparison with plants with sufficient nitrogen.

Remedy: Use either sulphate of ammonia (1 oz in two gals) or ammonium nitrate (1oz in five gals), once a week for three weeks, as quick acting suppliers of nitrogen. Dried blood (one application at 2oz per plant for a three to five-year-old plant) is a good organic nitrogen booster.

Nitrogen excess: Lush growth, with larger, thinner leaves than normal. Late summer growth may fail to mature and be vulnerable to winter frost damage to leaves and shoots. Bark splitting is also likely to occur after cold weather.

Phosphorus (P) Most fertilizers supply this element in its superphosphate form. This is insoluble in water, so it needs to be broken down in the soil (a complex process beyond the scope of this book to describe) into chemical components which plants are able take up and use. This is a slow process, which explains why phosphorus is more persistent and remains in the soil when nitrates and potassium salts have been used or washed away. Phosphorus is also less mobile in the soil.

Apart from the traditionally accepted role of building proteins, thus encouraging good root systems, phosphorus is also used, together with magnesium and others minerals in the everyday activity of plant cells. It is significant in the transfer of energy for sugar manufacture in the leaves.

Superphosphate has no effect on the acidity or alkalinity of the soil.

Phosphorus excess: more commonly seen in young plants in containers during the winter or early spring. Leaves turn a deep chocolate brown before falling off. If detected early enough the soil should be flushed through with clear water.

Potassium (K). This is an interactive element, working closely with others in the day-to-day functions of the plant. It is very mobile within plants.

Deficiency: First noticeable in older leaves, as potassium moves out of them to the more demanding growing tips of shoots at times of shortage. Leaves develop a bluish green colour, often with black speckling between the leaf veins. Symptoms of leaf scorch follow, followed by leaf drop.

Remedy: Potassium sulphate (1oz in 2 gallons of water), should be used once a week for three weeks, as a corrective measure. Good soil conditions and the use of a balanced fertilizer should avoid the problem in future.

Magnesium (Mg). This element is vital in the

making and use of chlorophyll, which not only gives plants their green colouring, but is essential in the energy transfer during sugar manufacture in the leaves. It is also important in the production of healthy camellia flowers.

Deficiency: Paleness (chlorosis) between the leaf veins in older leaves, often with orange/yellow patches developing. (The variety C. M. Hovey seems prone to this.) Camellias on poor, over-acidic soils, whether clay or sandy, are more likely to show these symptoms. Poor flower formation is another symptom.

Remedy: Magnesium limestone, in powdered form for quicker action, not only corrects the deficiency, but also neutralises acid conditions which in itself helps camellias to absorb magnesium salts. Two to 3oz per square yard is a general recommendation.

Calcium (Ca). Although camellias do not thrive in calcium-rich soils, they do need traces of this element for construction of cell walls and the building of plant tissues. Calcium is not available in very acid conditions; its optimum availability is over pH6 so symptoms are seen more often on camellias growing in acidic, sandy soils.

Deficiency: Symptoms are most often seen on young shoots and leaves which have been physically damaged, for example, where a late spring frost has scorched them, causing 'tip burn'. The deficiency is localised in the young leaves, which have blackened margins. These leaves never recover, and always remain pinched and small.

Remedy: For an effect over a reasonably long period (a year or two) scatter 2-4oz of various sizes of of limestone chippings per square yard if the soil tests at pH4 or less. Test the pH before being tempted to repeat the application.

Iron (Fe). Iron rich soils seem to suit camellias,

with extra rich flower colours being produced. This is because iron is used in pigment formation, both in flowers and leaves. It is vital in the formation of chlorophyll (but not as an ingredient). It is active in acidic soils, but chemically 'locked up' in alkaline conditions.

Deficiency: Young leaves are affected first, with chlorosis between the veins. This spreads if the deficiency is not corrected until whole leaves become almost white and the veins are no longer clearly visible. Brown patches or holes may appear along the leaf margins. Flowers tend to be pale and wishy washy.

Remedy: This is the situation when sequestered iron or 'sequestrine' is of value. It not only replaces the missing iron, but also, as a result, chemically unlocks other essential elements, such as potassium, which are closely linked in activity.

Sulphur (S). The amount of sulphur present in plants sometimes exceeds the amount of phosphorus. It is needed in pigment formation, chlorophyll and for growth.

Deficiency: Pale leaves, with short spaces (internodes) between them. Seen on camellias growing in alkaline soils.

Remedy: Correction of the alkalinity, followed by the use of a balanced fertilizer which includes trace elements, should do the trick. Flowers of sulphur may also be used, but with great care taken to follow packet instructions.

Aluminium (Al) and **molybdenum** (Mb). These both affect colour. Tests have shown that red flowers will sometimes deepen to purple if these minerals are added to soil. Soils with a high proportion of clay are often rich in aluminium and varieties such as *C. japonica* 'Dona Herzilia de Freitas Magalhaes' and 'Zambo' are only really truly purple in these soils.

Which fertilizer?

Bearing in mind the general requirement of camellias for a higher percentage of nitrogen in spring and a lower nitrogen content towards the end of the growing season, the choice of fertilizers is fairly straightforward. Deciding upon liquid feeding, or top dressing with a granular or pelleted fertilizer is up to the individual. Liquid feeding is more controlled and accurate and frequently used for container-grown camellias, especially if there are few. Regular application, on a weekly or fortnightly basis according to the brand used, will be needed. Top dressing with a granular or controlled release fertilizer is less accurate, but less demanding on time. It is the usual method for camellias in the garden borders and is also successful for containers. It is usually a twice-a-growing-season job.

Types of fertilizer

For liquid feeding in the UK: N:P:K analyses:

Chempak 3 – 20:20:20

J. Arthur Bowers (ericaceous) – 5.0 : 4.0 : 7.0 (plus wetting agent)

Maxicrop – 5.1 : 5.1 : 6.7

For top dressing, granular, feeding in the UK: N:P:K analyses:

Growmore – 7.0 : 7.0 : 7.0

Vitax Q4 – 5.3 : 7.5 : 10.0 (a little low in N, especially on poor, sandy soils where nitrogen may be used or leached out too soon).

Organic fertilizer for summer feeding: fish blood and bone (sterilised) – 5.0 : 5.0 : 6.5

Controlled-release fertilizer pellets are now widely available and extremely useful, not only to incorporate in compost before potting, but also as a top dressing. The most widely available is probably Osmocote, 14 : 13 :13. It releases nutrients gently over a six-month period, with virtually no release in cold climate winters. If the average temperature over the six months is 21°C it will run out in that time, but will last longer if the average is lower.

Wetting agents are gels which reduce water loss by evaporation. They contribute no nutrients, but are included in some fertilizer formulations as a useful additive.

Some additional comments:

1. Fertilizers with a high percentage of phosphorus (e.g: N (15) : P (30) : K (15)), may cause root scorch, especially if used on a soil which is already phosphate rich.

    Acidifying fertilizers are useful where soil or compost tends towards the alkaline – where the pH is above 6.2 – but not recommended if the soil is already acidic. Their use on camellias in peat-based composts is particularly undesirable.

    Products sold as Sequestered Iron, sometimes with magnesium and/or manganese added, supply just those minerals and should be used if camellias are showing deficiencies. They are often used to good effect in soils with a high pH because they chemically 'unlock' nutrients previously unavailable because of the alkalinity. They do not supply the major minerals N, P, or K, so they cannot be termed 'a food' for camellias.

    Fertilizers formulated for bedding plants, hanging baskets, etc, tend to be short term in action and generally too low in nutrient levels, especially nitrogen, for camellias.

    There is no evidence that camellias absorb fertilizer through the leaves. They have a waxy upper surface, however, which encourages rapid run-off of moisture and the leaves conduct this down to the roots in a very effective manner.

Timing

Spring feeding

Look for an analysis similar to: N (10%) : P (7.5%) : K (10%) (in the UK this is found in the granular Vitax formulation for conifers, etc, plus azaleas and rhododendrons). For liquid feeding the analysis : N (25%) : P (15%) : K (15%) is found in the Chempak 2. Magnesium, iron and possibly other elements may be included. Dried blood provides a high nitrogen organic alternative.

For summer feeding in order to both keep up with the demands of actively growing camellias and to encourage flower buds to form and to develop, it may be necessary to change to a fertilizer with a more balanced formulation. There are plenty available. If using liquid fertilizer, or a top dressing of a granular one, the first feed of the year needs to be given towards the end of the spring flowering period when growth is about to start. Later feeding should boost later flushes of growth (one more in cold climates, two or even three in warmer areas).

All feeding should end when camellias stop needing it, when they have become almost inactive; ie. it should cease a few weeks before growth stops. The time depends on the climate, and the condition of the plants. They should go into the winter in a healthy, glossy, green state with firm, well ripened shoot tips. This is particularly important in cold climates.

Winter feeding can be wasteful because camellias simply do not need minerals at that time, so they are just washed out of the soil. It can also actually harm camellias, especially small ones or those in dry soil, by causing root scorch. (Reverse osmosis occurs: the chemical solution in the soil is more concentrated than that inside the root cells so water is drawn out of, instead of into, the roots, in order to try to get a balance.)

Caution: When using any chemical the manufacturer's instructions should be read and understood, particularly those referring to safety. Hands should be washed thoroughly after using any chemical.

Pruning – general principles and methods

Note: sharp knives or secateurs and, where needed, saws should always be used.

Left to their own devices camellias purchased as small plants will grow to their own natural size and shape, with great variation according to variety and the situation in the garden, both climatic and soil. Some, such as 'Donation' may reach five metres or more in both height and width in about 20 years which is fine if space is unlimited, but rather a problem if the garden is relatively small. Others are naturally compact, tidy growers and can be left alone, except for the odd tidy-up of stray branches.

The answer when space is limited is to prune annually from an early age, to shape and control as required. If this is done the plants will always look pleasing and 'natural'. If things get out of hand and major surgery is required then this may be carried out, but it leaves the bushes looking unbalanced and ugly for two or three years until they recover.

Before deciding on the method of pruning to use it might be worth considering personal requirements. Are the camellias to be kept as a collection, possibly in order to have blooms for showing, with no importance given to the visual appearance of the plants? Or do they form part of a garden display where their overall appearance matters? What lateral space will they ultimately be allowed, and am I prepared to move them if they later appear too crowded, rather than control them as they grow?

Pruning young camellias

The pruning policy for young plants is to form the future foundation for growth, with the aim of creating a shapely plant which will be pleasing to the eye in all seasons.

When first purchased, camellia plants will either be tall and thinly furnished, trained up a cane, or will be self-supporting and already multi-branched and of bushy appearance due to the fact that they have been shaped from an early age in the nursery. Both will, if left alone, branch out and find their own shape in time. If the camellia has already been shaped, the only work to be done is to carry on where the nursery left off and to maintain the shape as it grows. The former involves more work, and such plants may need to be cut right back in their first year if bushiness is required from low down. Each plant should have a single main stem which is obviously dominant and the plant should be maintained that way. A camellia with two 'leaders' is vulnerable to splitting in two later on, especially in areas where snow is likely. The V shape made by such a junction is also an open invitation for water to accumulate, and future fungal attack and subsequent rotting is very likely.

It is always a good idea to cut back to just above a leaf axil which has what appears to be a healthy bud between leaf stalk and stem, and two or more further leaf axils with buds ready to grow out, behind that. This way there should be three shoots in a few weeks time where there was only one before.

The technique is to cut back to the point behind which new shoots are required to grow and to look for points behind which there are at least two likely buds, or even to take out all of the last shoot, cutting just above the junction of this and the previous growth, where there will be multiple buds. The trick is to look ahead and visualise what the camellia will look like when the buds which can be seen in axils behind the cut have grown out into shoots.

In all but the coldest areas there will be at least two spells of vegetative growth and the first pruning should be just before the first spell, in spring. This will be just as flowering comes to an end, if there are any, and the last few flowers may have to be sacrificed and brought indoors to be enjoyed as cut flowers.

After this the young shoots should grow quickly. If the camellia is of an open habit and a more bushy plant is required then the tips of this young growth may be pinched out, or even removed entirely, to encourage further branching in the second spell of growth. This may produce an over dense plant in varieties which are naturally bushy and slow growing so these should not be pinched out. Bushiness right down to ground level is not advised where conditions are likely to be damp and humid as bark rot may be encouraged. Branches should start from several centimetres up the main stem in these conditions, with allowance for the fact that the stem will elongate and fill out as time passes.

A third period of growth may follow the second growth spell in warm climates.

After this flower buds should form on the first growth.

Insulation:

Insulating a large pot or tub

Insulation:

Insulating a small container

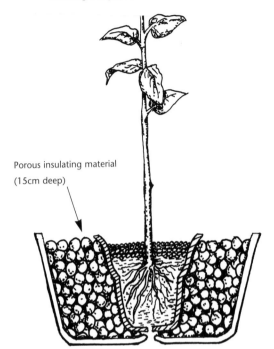
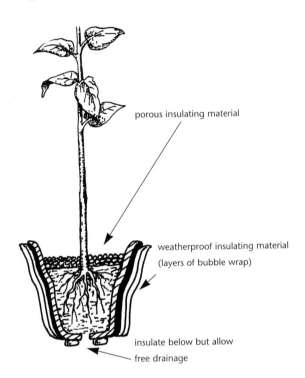

porous insulating material

Porous insulating material
(15cm deep)

weatherproof insulating material
(layers of bubble wrap)

insulate below but allow
free drainage

Unrooted cutting grafting:

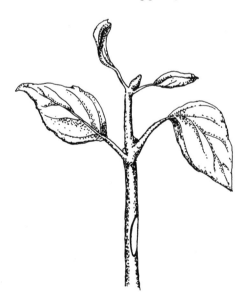

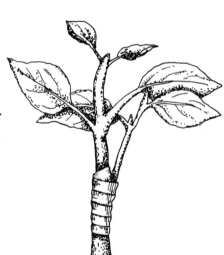

Unrooted rootstock prepared to
receive scion

Scion with one slide sliced
clearly to match stock

Stock and scion united and ready to
insert into rooting medium

Pruning mature camellias

Camellias which have reached the stage where
they have obviously woody branches and a more
mature appearance with the overall shape well
established, should be producing a good show of
flowers and need to be maintained in order keep
this up and to display them to best advantage.
Pruning encourages vegetative growth, not
flowers, so this must be remembered.

The first thing to do is to stand back, view the
camellia objectively, and make some basic
decisions about what needs to be done.
Obviously any dead or diseased wood comes out
first, then wayward branches which are growing
too vigorously in relation to the rest, and maybe
the top leader if the bush has reached the size
required. After that it may be that the centre of
the bush is deemed too dense and branches are
crowded so much that not only are blooms
squashed and spoilt, but branches are prone to
disease, especially die-back. This is a problem in
parts of New Zealand and Australia and other
areas where humidity can be high. Here the
saying is that 'camellias should be pruned ìso
that a bird can fly through them'. In Britain we
tend not to bother so much, but it is a good idea
to thin branches every now and again to avoid
overcrowding, especially in varieties such as
'Anticipation' which has a very dense habit and
large blooms.

Drastic surgery

One of the biggest concerns for the future is what
will happen to all those unpruned camellias
which have grown so big that they are now a
burden to their owners instead of a pleasure ? It
is not uncommon to see huge plants filling the
whole of a front garden, or obscuring the view
from a window completely, or a group of very
sparse, tall camellias with flowers only at the top

Camellias which have been pruned hard soon recover and
produce healthy shoots from bare branches

where they can hardly be seen. These are
liabilities which need never have happened, but
the situation can be easily resolved.

Dense plants can be 'hat racked', with the
majority of branches sawn back hard. This
should be done in late winter or early spring
before the sap rises and growth starts.
Any camellia, and certainly the tall, sparse ones,
can be cut almost to ground level at the same
time of year.

Camellias which have received major surgery

This front door scene in New Zealand is enhanced by a standard 'Snowdrop' and the dwarf, bushy plant of 'Baby Bear'

will, like any patient, take time to recover, and it is likely to be after mid-summer before there is any sign of life from the woody stumps. Just when all hope has gone small buds will appear on the bare wood, and they will rapidly grow out into a multitude of twiggy branches which promise a handsome bushy plant for the future. From then on the same principles of pruning apply as before, with the resolution that never again will a camellia be allowed to dominate its owner !

Speciality pruning techniques

It is possible to train camellias to all sorts of shapes. Fans and espaliers can cover unsightly walls, standards or half standards can grace formal areas, hanging baskets can have naturally cascading varieties tumbling from them, and the intricacies of bonsai can be explored. (For container-growth pruning see pg 88.)

Standards

Growing camellias as 'standards' is a practice which has been around for a long time, but is little publicised, probably because few nurseries have the resources to carry out the initial training. It is quite easy to do, but takes time and is well worth the effort.

Standard camellias, unlike standard roses, are attractive all year round and enhance a formal setting, particularly where space is too limited for a more free growing camellia. Standards may either be grown from scions of the chosen variety grafted on to a strong upright stock at a selected height, or grown as a single variety on its own roots.

The initial selection of a suitable camellia is the most important thing. If grown on its own roots it has to be one which lends itself to being trained from a single straight, strong stem, so it has to be of a variety which is either naturally upright and vigorous, such as 'Spring Festival' or throws out long, strong growth such as 'Mary Phoebe Taylor'. Cascading camellias like 'Taroan' ('Yoibijin') or even 'Elegant Beauty' also make good subjects, but are better used as grafts on more naturally robust, upright growers as their main stems may not be sufficiently strong to form good standards. (Grafting techniques are described on page 84.)

A camellia on its own roots, purchased as an ordinary plant with a single strong, straight stem, will need to have all its lateral branches removed up to a point above which the flowering part is to be concentrated. From then on any buds which appear on the stem should be rubbed off and the flowering area kept shapely by pruning and pinching out regularly. A stake will be needed for young plants and maybe for larger camellias particularly if the top is likely to be heavy.

Hanging baskets

These can be grown outdoors all year round in warm climates, but will need to be kept protected from frost in colder areas as the root system is particularly restricted and vulnerable to frost damage. They make excellent conservatory plants, especially if scented varieties such as 'Spring Mist' or 'Quintessence' or 'Sweet Emily Kate' are chosen to give added value.

Small-leaved, slow growing, small flowered varieties with a spreading or cascading habit make the best subjects and it is better to start off with a small plant of about two years old. Any hanging basket design may be chosen, but the pot type with inbuilt saucer below is more popular than the true basket. A normal ericaceous compost should be used, but care should be taken to avoid high nitrogen feeds which stimulate over vigorous growth. Regular watering is especially

'Fairy Wand' makes an interesting hanging basket in the warm climate of New Zealand

important in a container suspended above ground with free air circulation around it, and the use of a water-retaining gel is highly recommended. Training will be a combination of regular pinching out and pruning to keep size and shape under control, combined with weight training in the growing season. This involves tying weights to branches which need to be encouraged to grow laterally and slightly downwards, using strips of soft fabric such as old nylon stockings, but not string which will cut into them. If these weights are used on branches from the previous years growth which are firm but still 'whippy', during the summer they will be firmly directed by the following winter. They are then removed in order to enjoy the flowers. This process may need to be repeated for one or two more summers, by which time the shape will be well established and the camellia will then need just regular pruning for

the rest of its four or five more years in its basket. It is then time to remove it and use it as a cascading feature in an attractive urn on the ground, or tumbling over a boulder or bank outdoors if the variety is hardy enough.

Bonsai

This is the ultimate in controlled container growing and is a very specialist subject. As with all camellias, the containers must be kept frost free in winter.

Varieties with small leaves and flowers will be more suitable for small containers, but any variety may be chosen for large containers, with low growing, spreading camellias such as 'Elegans' being popular.

Young plants which show promise of an interesting shape, possibly those which have been put out as rejects by the nursery because of a

Camellias in a bonsai collection in Auckland

crooked stem, are ideal, especially if they are stocky and well branched near the base – plants of character rather than conventional good looks. They should be removed from the pot, the roots examined and any dominant root removed – as a system of fine fibrous roots near the surface of the soil is to be encouraged – then repotted and grown for one more year before putting into the chosen bonsai container. These are available from specialist suppliers or the local bonsai society. These societies have very knowledgeable members who will help with the finer points of bonsai culture. The basic points are to contain the roots initially by pruning, feeding little and often, watering frequently, and to control the vegetative growth by pinching out regularly in the summer. Shapes can be encouraged by using fabric-covered wire to twist and tie branches into the desired positions.

PROPAGATION

Camellia propagation can be rewarding and fun for those who have patience and a slight spirit of adventure; those who are prepared to gamble a little. Camellia varieties do not 'come true' from seed, so it is necessary to use a vegetative method in order to reproduce the chosen cultivars. Propagation may be by grafting, layering or cuttings, depending on the facilities available.

Propagation by cuttings

This is now by far the most important method of propagation used both by commercial camellia growers and at home. Home propagators of many shapes and sizes are now widely available to plug into the glasshouse power supply while many green-fingered folk have success simply by using ordinary plant pots in the house. It might take up to a year to root the cuttings with this basic equipment but patience often pays off. Some camellias root more easily than others; it is a very varietal business, with the C. *reticulata* varieties and hybrids being the most difficult along with any that are virus-infected (mottled flowers like 'Anticipation variegated').

Pot propagation

The simplest propagator is a fairly shallow plant pot, with sufficient holes to allow good drainage. This is essential as the compost must be kept moist but never wet. The bathroom or kitchen windowsill is a popular place for the pot, to give good light but not direct sunlight.

Since cuttings are leafy stems deprived of their roots, until they make their own, they have to take water up as best they can, sufficient to prevent wilting and also to keep the leaves actively manufacturing food. There is insufficient uptake to cope with the usual water loss (transpiration), so this must be prevented by creating an atmosphere of 100% humidity around the shoot. The simplest method is to make a mini-polythene house by inverting a polythene bag over the pot. It can then be held in place with a rubber band or string, and kept clear of contact with the cuttings by using three sticks. (A quick puff of breath will inflate the bag and will also add a little extra carbon dioxide, which is beneficial.)

Another method is to cut the bottom off a plastic lemonade or soda bottle and to use the top half as a pot cover. The screw top needs to be kept on to start with, but can be removed after rooting as the first stage of hardening-off.

Propagation kits

Commercially made propagation kits are available and are well worth having if a large number of plants are to be propagated. Those which have a mist unit are excellent especially for summer propagation. They speed up rooting by keeping the cuttings cool as well as 100% humid. Care has to be taken to avoid the compost becoming too wet in the hottest weather when the mist may be almost continuous. It should be turned off at night.

Home propagators can also include heating cables or mats which can be thermostatically controlled to keep the temperature in the propagating trays at the optimum 17 to 20°C. This is especially useful for winter propagation. Fairly heavy shade will also be needed if direct sunlight is likely to reach the propagation area, not only to keep the cuttings cool, but also to prevent the sun scorching the leaves.

Rooting media

Various materials are used as a rooting medium to insert the cuttings into, with each skilled propagator swearing by his/her own special mix, but the following is a well tried and tested combination. As much as 75% gritty sand to 25% peat (by volume) seems to suit both camellias and azaleas. (Seaside sand is not recommended as it usually contains a high proportion of ground up, chalky seashells.) The sand ensures that the mix is well drained and has plenty of air to keep it sweet, while the peat holds on to sufficient moisture to keep it damp. Polystyrene granules, perlite, or vermiculite may all be used instead of sand. There are also several brands of commercially prepared seed and cutting composts available but these are more suitable for short-term subjects such as fuchsias and chrysanthemums.

Hormone rooting powder or liquid is not always essential in warm climates but, properly used, certainly encourages rooting, and is

regarded as a must for autumn and winter cuttings in cold climate areas. There are a number on the market, both powder and liquid, to suit both semi-hardwood and hardwood cuttings. Directions should be closely followed as excess hormone can inhibit or even prevent rooting.

Selection, preparation and care of cuttings

Whatever the facilities, the selection and preparation of cuttings is the same.

Two types of cutting may be used: semi-hardwood and hard-wood. The former are taken when young growth is just firm but the young shoots have just turned brown but have not yet become woody. They become available in both late summer and in autumn, after each flush of growth. Firmer (hardwood) cuttings are taken in winter when the plants are dormant and the shoots from the previous growing season have ripened and have just become hard and woody. The latter take longer to root; 12 weeks at least, while the former, particularly those taken early, may take as little as six weeks in ideal conditions, but more often nine to 12 weeks in a modern propagator, more in a pot at home.

Different parts of the stem may be used to provide:

- Terminal or tip cuttings, with or without heels
- Stem cuttings
- Bud cuttings

Terminal cuttings, where about 10cm of the top of a healthy young shoot is used, are preferable as they grow into nice balanced plants more quickly, while stem cuttings, taken from a similar-sized section lower down, tend to have long spaces between buds (internodes), and care needs to be

Rooted cuttings in cell
trays under plastic

Seedlings beginning to
grow in their pan, which
was kept in a galvanised
container to keep mice
out

taken later to avoid producing a plant with two
leading shoots which have a point of weakness
between them, where the camellia can more easily
be damaged by debris accumulating and rotting,
or by splitting in a gale, etc.

Bud cuttings, when a much smaller piece of
stem is taken, with one bud in the axil of a leaf,
are usually used when propagating material is
scarce, but although more plants can be produced
from each shoot it will take a little longer for
each to grow into a sizeable plant.

Collection of cuttings

All cuttings should be taken from healthy, green,

Ready to start
propagation

Prepared cuttings of a large-leafed camellia, dipped in hormone powder

preferably youngish plants as 'juvenile' growth makes the best cuttings, which root well.

Cutting material should be taken in early morning, in the cool of the evening, or on a dull cool day, placed immediately in a polythene bag and a spray of cool water given before tying the bag to keep the atmosphere moist. Each variety will need to be labelled. One method, particularly when only one or two cuttings are taken, is to use a waterproof pen to write the name on the back of one of the leaves of each cutting. Another is to tie cuttings into bundles of each variety using string or secure rubber bands, and to insert a label into the bundle. Yet another is to use a single polythene bag for each variety and a waterproof pen to write its name on the bag or on a label inside it. The most important thing is to keep the cuttings moist and cool until they can be prepared and inserted into the propagating medium.

If soil warming is being used it should be checked in advance, to see that all is well (including the thermostat) and turned on a day or so before use to get the soil up to temperature before the cuttings are inserted.

Preparation of cuttings

When all is ready, and the propagating medium has had a good soak and been allowed to drain

Cuttings inserted in their rooting medium

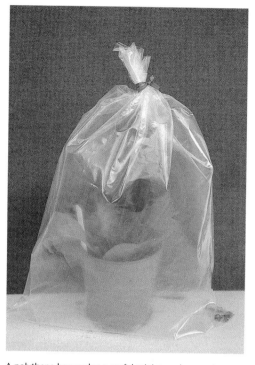

A polythene bag makes a useful mini-greenhouse when 100 percent humidity can be maintained

off all excess water, it is time to prepare and insert the cuttings.

A very sharp knife is needed. Stanley knives, available in hardware stores everywhere, are excellent.

Cuttings of the chosen type are prepared, making sure that all cuts are trimmed cleanly, including neatening-off the heels of those which have them. The bottom cut always used to be below a node or leaf joint, although this is no longer considered essential, but lower leaves should be removed. Small-leaved varieties can have three or four leaves left, larger ones two or three. It is preferable to leave these leaves intact, partly because it gives a better total surface area of leaf for photosynthesis, and partly because any cut surface is an invitation to fungal spores. Very large leaves will, however, have to be sliced as these cuttings tend to push each other out of

Left to right: a) rooted cutting ready for potting b) at the end of its first year's growth c) at the end of its second year's growth

the propagator. Each cutting has a 1cm wound made at the base to expose the cambium tissue underneath the bark.

Using plastic or rubber gloves to protect the hands the prepared cuttings may then be dipped in a suitable fungicide. (It is impossible to recommend one here as regulations change so rapidly in all countries, and old favourites are removed from the 'Approved lists' to be replaced by new ones.) Excess chemical needs to be shaken off, and then the prepared lower end dipped in hormone rooting liquid or powder before being inserted in the rooting medium.

Commercially there is no time to use a dibber; the cuttings are just pushed into the compost, but most home propagators use a dibber to make a hole for each cutting, taking care to push the compost close to the cutting afterwards. Cuttings can be put in as close as you like; they will help to keep each other moist, but three or 4cm apart is about right. They are then well watered in, allowed to drain thoroughly, the mist unit turned on, or the plastic covers placed in position.

It does not matter if the air temperature under the polythene rises to 40°C briefly in short hot spells, as long as there is some shade, but it is quite easy to cool things down by hosing the polythene sheeting down with cold water two or three times a day when possible. The fungicide dip should have controlled any potential fungal attack, but resistant spores may develop, so a watch should be kept for signs of *Botrytis* in particular and any dropped leaves must be removed as soon as they are seen.

After about four weeks in ideal conditions there should be some callus beginning to form on some of the cuttings – it will not hurt to have a look. (In fact, one of the methods used to encourage rooting of some of the more difficult

Vaccinium species is to remove them deliberately to trim the callus and then to re-position them.) After another two to three weeks the first roots may begin to grow out from the callus, and from then on the root system develops rapidly. The timing varies widely from variety to variety, from season to season and from year to year. The rooted cuttings can either be potted up as soon as they are sufficiently rooted, if ready in late summer or early autumn, or if it is late autumn or winter they are probably best left undisturbed in the glasshouse, protected from frost.

In the spring the cuttings can be potted up into an ericaceous or general-purpose compost. If a tap root has developed it should be cut to encourage lateral branching instead. Young plants need to be kept in a protected environment under glass in a cold climate, or lathe house in a hot one, for another year, kept fed, watered and if necessary pruned and shaped before being potted and grown until ready for planting out at three or four years old in cold climates, younger in more clement conditions.

Grafting

Grafting is the traditional way to propagate camellias, practised by the Chinese for centuries before camellias reached Europe and the rest of the world. Approach grafting, where small stock plants growing in their pots are tied close to scions of the variety to be propagated still attached to their large camellia bush or tree, is still practised in some parts of China today, although it is no longer practised elsewhere.

Cleft grafting is the most usual, although, for those with rooting facilities for cuttings, the newer cutting graft method is very rewarding. Although propagation by cuttings is now the most widely used method, there is still a place for grafting, using these and other less common methods. Some varieties, such as *C. japonica* 'Augusto Leal de Gouveia Pinto' and some of the *C. reticulatas* like 'Captain Rawes' and 'Robert Fortune' are very difficult to root.

Also, in areas where *Phytopthora* root rot is a problem it is sometimes advantageous to graft the required varieties onto *C.sasanqua* rootstocks as this species is resistant to *Phytopthora*, as are its cultivars and hybrids.

Cultivars of many species backgrounds have been found to be compatible. Varieties of *C. japonica*, *C. reticulata*, *C. sasanqua* and hybrids of all sorts are all grafted onto *C. sasanqua* rootstocks with success, but it needs to be born in mind that *C. sasanqua* root systems are sometimes particularly prone to frost damage.

Two more reasons come to mind: a larger plant can be achieved in a short time by grafting a scion on a vigorous rootstock. For example if a scion of the chosen variety is grafted onto a substantial, say, metre high, five or six-year-old understock, the scion should reach the size of the original understock in one year, especially in good climates as in Australia or New Zealand, and under glass elsewhere. It is also sometimes easier for a home gardener to propagate from grafts than from cuttings if he/she does not have proper facilities for rooting cuttings. On the down side, it is often difficult, especially in countries like Britain where camellias do not set seed very readily, to find enough suitable young plants to act as stock plants to graft onto. The other, more long-term disadvantage is that the rootstock frequently produces the odd bud from below the union and this grows up through the foliage of the chosen variety grafted onto it, and if left in place may well dominate it. It should be removed as soon as it appears.

Cleft grafting

The time to do this is ideally in mid-winter, but any time in the dormant season will do.

Materials required: Young, strong, stock plants, traditionally two to three years old with a single stem of about pencil thickness or a little more, although much older plants with much bigger diameters and without branches for a few centimetres above soil level, are fine for growing in containers. Healthy, discarded seedlings, especially of *C. sasanqua* are ideal, but any healthy vigorous plant of whatever is available will do for most scions in most areas. *C. reticulata* varieties and hybrids were once thought to be best grafted onto *C. reticulatas*, but they have been found to be quite happy on other stock, especially on the *C. sasanqua* mentioned earlier.

Equipment needed includes: secateurs, a very sharp knife (a Stanley knife is ideal), grafting tape (plastic plumbers' tape is fine), sharp sand, old, two-litre size, plastic lemonade bottles, with the bottom cut off to give the size needed to cover the finished graft and leave some clearance for growth, or a plastic bag to be held above by sticks, to be secured to the pot by string or elastic band. Add a small screwdriver with the top filed to make it really slim, some hormone rooting liquid or powder, fungicide, a lens, and a label for each plant.

Most commercial growers now do without grafting tape as long as they have skilled staff to ensure that the scion is well and truly wedged in the cleft of the stock, and few bother with hormone or fungicides.

In the past the stock plants were always kept on the dry side for a few days prior to being used because composts used to be much heavier, containing loam which holds water and tends to lack air. When the foliage from the stock is

Cleft grafting:

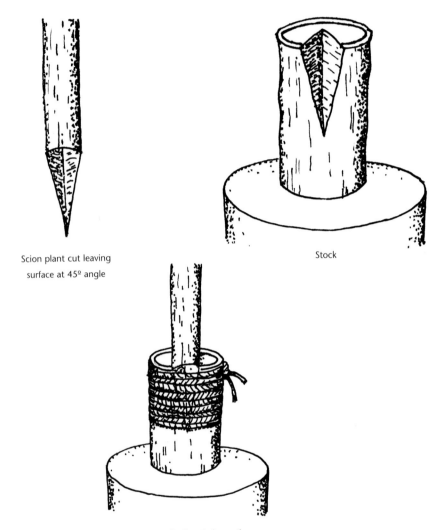

Scion plant cut leaving
surface at 45º angle

Stock

Stock and scion tied together
(Layers just under the bark of stock and scion in contact)

removed water uptake is drastically reduced, encouraging sourness in the compost and consequent root rot. With modern composts which have more air pockets and are more free draining this does not matter, so drying out is not necessary. The compost should be moist and all weeds cleaned off. A layer of sharp sand is sometimes added to the compost surface, but is not essential. Lower leaves are then removed up to the desired grafting height, about 8cm is traditional, but a lower graft leaves less room for the development of buds from the wood of the stock. The top of the plant is removed, using a very sharp pair of secateurs to cut at an angle of about 45º. A sharp knife is then used to trim off any untidy or bruised surfaces. Next, the knife is used to split the stock vertically down the centre to about 2cm in preparation for receiving the scion.

The scion is taken and prepared by removing the lower leaf, then, using the very sharp knife, the bottom of the scion is made into a double wedge shape. The stock and scion are then ready for putting together.

Using the narrow-ended screwdriver, the vertical cut on the stock plant is prised open and the scion gently put in place so that the layers of cambium cells of both stock and scion are in contact with each other. If necessary, a lens can be used to check this; look to see that the thin layer of cells just under the bark of both is in contact down the outside edge. The top of the cut surfaces of the scion may be just slightly raised above the stock at the finish to encourage good callusing over the top of the union in the future, but this is not essential. The two may then be bound together using plastic tape, if used, and perhaps given a fine spray over with fungicide, taking care not to overdo it, before putting the clean ex-lemonade bottle or other cover over. If this is pushed into the sand with a slight screwing motion it will ensure a good seal.

The newly grafted plant is then put into a frost-free glasshouse with shade netting or other shade material, and left undisturbed. After about six weeks the scion should have a perky look about it and some callus should be forming between it and the stock. After eight weeks, especially if the weather is now getting warmer, the union should be completely calloused, and callus visible at the top of it. By ten weeks the bottom of each jar can be raised a little to give some ventilation, with more being gradually given until, after another week or ten days the jars are completely removed. The shade should, however, remain in place. This is a critical period as new growth will now be apparent and this can collapse so easily during weaning, especially in

hot weather. If this happens give the foliage a spray of cold water and replace the jar.

During all this time there will probably be no need to water the plants as there is so little uptake, but they should never be allowed to dry out. As the scion grows and the weather warms up, the pot should be watered more as demand increases, and in hot weather the foliage of the young plant sprayed over with cold water too. Plenty of shade is needed for the whole of the first growing season because, as with any patient recovering from a major operation, it takes time for the plant to heal and to take up water sufficiently effectively to cope with rapid transpiration in hot sunny conditions.

Cleft grafting may be carried out in order to create a 'standard'. Once a suitable stock plant has reached its desired height it can be severed in the usual way and the chosen scion grafted onto it. A wire framework can be constructed over the area. Damp sphagnum moss is tied just below the graft to create the humid atmosphere needed, and a plastic bag fixed firmly over the wire, tying it securely to the stock to make a seal. The plant is then kept in a frost free, shaded area, and treated as before. This is not an easy operation, but it can be fun to have a go. Some greenery left up the stem of the stock to help pull the sap up might be beneficial until the scion has started to grow away well.

Cutting grafts

This more recent method is worth trying for those who have efficient propagators for cuttings. The two main advantages are that it is not necessary to spend several years growing stock plants, and, since the union is so low, there is less room for buds to break from the stock. Also the union is much neater and less visible because the grafting is done low and at such a young age. The principle behind it is the grafting of a difficult to root variety onto an easy to root one, resistant to root rot for preference, at the semi-hardwood cuttings stage.

C. *sasanqua* or an easy-to-root camellia of any cultivar is used as the under stock cutting, choosing terminal growth or a stem cutting in the normal way, and trimming the lower leaves off both as usual and squaring off the lower cut surface of the stock neatly.

The chosen scion, which should be about the same diameter as the stock, is then prepared. It is usually a little shorter than the stock. The lower end of the scion should be cut into a wedge shape, as for cleft grafting, and the stock gently bent to open the slit to allow the scion to be carefully inserted, making sure the layers of cambium tissue are in contact. A rubber band or tape is used to hold the two together and the resultant cutting is put into the propagator and treated as any other cutting, with the union about 2cm below the surface of the propagating medium. To avoid confusion, especially if stock and cutting have similar leaves, the stock is always left with three leaves and the scion with two.

Once the stock is well rooted its top can be cut off with a sharp knife, as closely and neatly as possible, and the new plant potted up and cared for in the normal way.

The above methods are the most commonly used in modern camellia cultivation, but the ancient Chinese method of Approach grafting is still widely used in China today. It involves the use of a well established parent plant which will provide the chosen scion. A suitable stock plant, usually a seedling in a pot, provides the root system. The stock plant is then placed and firmly secured, so that it is close enough for the selected young shoot of the scion to be 'married' to the stem of the stock.

Propagation by layering
Root layering
This occurs naturally when a low growing branch becomes gradually covered by leaf litter and, if left undisturbed, throws out adventitious roots (roots which arise directly from a stem). The C. *rusticana* (Snow Camellias) form dense, spreading thickets in this way.

Other camellias can be encouraged to form new plants in this way by wounding the underside of a low branch to expose the cambium cells beneath the bark just below a small branch, or bud, then pegging the wounded branch down on either side of the wound, and covering it with leaf litter which should remain damp. Roots will grow out into the soil during the summer and the resultant small plant can then be severed from the parent. It can then be potted up into normal ericaceous compost, without too much disturbance to the roots, and left to grow in the normal way.

Air layering
This follows the same method but branches above ground are used and it is a bit more fiddly. It can be a useful way of getting sizeable plants quite quickly from an otherwise difficult to propagate variety, especially if propagating facilities for cuttings are not available, or stock plants for grafting are not to hand. It is best done as soon as the bark is loose enough to lift, in early summer, and should produce roots and a new plant by autumn. Any young growth which is likely to wilt is best removed.

A healthy branch is selected, the top 45cm or so of which will be the new plant. Using a sharp knife, a ring of bark about 2cm wide is removed to expose the cambium cells below it. It should peel away easily as the bark is loose at this time of year. Rooting hormone may be painted onto

the wound or, if a powder, dusted on. A good
handful of sphagnum moss, which is available
from many florists, is dipped in water, squeezed
out to leave it damp but not dripping, and then
wrapped closely around the wound like a
bandage. To prevent drying out a piece of
polythene is wrapped firmly around this and tied
around the stem at each end of the parcel. It is
important to prevent rain trickling into the moss
down the branch, becoming trapped in the
polythene and forming a waterlogged, airless
pocket, which will prevent roots forming.
Provided a friendly environment of moisture and
air is maintained within the undisturbed parcel, a
good root system should be formed by autumn
when the new plant can be severed from the
parent by cutting just above and below the parcel
and the potential plant potted up in the usual
way, taking care to nurse it on under frost-free
protection during the first winter.

CONTAINERS AND BEDS

This section refers to plants which have got
beyond the rearing, nursery stage and are being
grown for their owners' intended enjoyment,
plants which have reached semi-maturity –
camellias of five years old or more.

There are many reasons why it may be
necessary or desirable to grow camellias in a
confined situation, in a tub, pot, or artificially
constructed bed. It may be that the garden soil is
alkaline and therefore totally unsuited to growing
any ericaceous plants, including camellias. Maybe
there is insufficient space left in the garden for
planting more camellias to add to a collection.
Maybe the addition of a few ornamental
containers with carefully selected, choice varieties
is deemed desirable to improve the ambience of a

terrace or yard. The placing of a special camellia
in a pot can add seasonal pleasure to a border
which is otherwise lacking interest at the time.
Containers are often grown under protection for
special displays; a well known gentleman who
visits his English racing stables for about four
days each spring delights in having his enormous
'specimen' camellias wheeled into his drawing
room to act as a highly decorative feature for the
duration of his short stay. A marvellous talking
point, but a nightmare for his gardeners to get the
timing of peak flowering accurate. This is not to
be recommended as general practice as the plants
suffer from the dry heat of a modern centrally
heated home and very soon drop first their flower
buds and then their leaves before collapsing
completely if left too long.

Many camellia enthusiasts who grow to
produce blooms for showing also use containers,
especially in the USA, where exhibiting in the
many camellia shows can be a full-time
occupation and is taken very seriously by the
really dedicated. It gives a degree of flexibility
and control of individual plants, which garden
growing does not.

Container growing is, however, more
demanding than growing in a garden situation
because the roots are restricted and unable to
spread sufficiently to take in water and nutrients
without help, and, of course, they are more
vulnerable to extremes of temperature.

The indoors/outdoors method
It is a common practice to keep camellias in their
containers outdoors in shade structures or other
suitable areas such as under trees or amongst
shrubs during the growing season, when it may be
quite hot, and often too hot in a small
glasshouse. The tubs or pots are then brought
into a glasshouse or conservatory for the winter

months, where the flowers can be enjoyed close at hand and in comfort for both owners and camellias. It is a system which gives the camellias the best of both worlds and allows the owners to fill their glasshouse etc. with other plants in summer. A host of home-made trolleys are used to help move large containers.

Containers kept permanently outdoors

Of course, it is not always necessary to move camellias into a protected environment for the winter; they can be grown all the year round outdoors in their tubs and pots, except in the few areas where it is impossible to lag the containers sufficiently to prevent freezing. Even then, many people simply bring their plants into a frost-proof shed or garage for the duration of the cold spell and put them back out again when it is over. This is an acceptable labour of love if relatively few plants of moderate size are involved, but can become too much of a burden when plants and containers are large and/or a considerable number of plants is involved. If this is the case then lagging of all plants is absolutely essential to prevent frost damage to the roots. Camellias in extra large tubs of 60cm or more may survive without root damage in periods of extended cold (-6°C, for a week or so), depending on wind chill. A 10cm deep mulch of coarse bark chippings, dried leaves or straw will be adequate protection. Ideally, this should be removed during the daytime if the sun's rays are sufficiently warm to have the effect of raising the temperature of the soil. Also ideally, the mulch should be replaced before nightfall to try to keep some of this warmth in, particularly if another few hours of chilling or freezing is expected. Other, smaller containers will not give this protection and should be lagged or brought into a frost-free area

before the onset of such weather.

Various methods are used to insulate containers. Smaller pots of less than about 20cm should either be plunged in soil in a sheltered spot under other larger shrubs, right up to their necks, or kept under glass, or plunged in soil in a cold frame.

Larger containers will need an insulating jacket before likely severe frost. This jacket needs to trap air to act as an insulator so something like plastic bin sacks loosely filled with straw, dried leaves or dead fern may be tied round. Alternatively, two or three layers of bubble polythene is efficient. It is better to use a waterproof material as a wet one replaces air with water, which is not an effective insulator and soon turns to ice as temperatures drop.

Varieties for container growing

A knowledge of the habit and natural growing speed of varieties under consideration helps, as does the knowledge that restriction of the roots in a container also acts as a curb to the growth above to a certain extent.

The choice of varieties is very personal and depends so much on the taste of the individuals involved and the purpose for which the camellias are to be grown. It may be that a collection of a particular type or group is to be made, in which case the growing habit will probably not be of great importance. On the other hand, if the camellias are to be grown primarily for their ornamental and aesthetic value they will probably need to be kept looking neat and tidy, in which case a rangy, vigorous variety will not be as desirable as a naturally bushy, slow growing type, although it is amazing how often the most beautiful flowers are found on untidy, wayward growers, which will need much more concentration on pruning to keep them under control.

Pruning container-grown camellias

Camellias grown in containers are frequently kept in a more formal shape than garden-grown ones, pruned to the size and shape desired by their owners, which is likely to mean a smaller bush than would be allowed in the border. It involves an annual or even twice-yearly job from the start, particularly if the less naturally compact growers are kept. It may be that a specially trained camellia is intended, perhaps a standard or maybe weeping varieties are favoured, or even one grown in a hanging basket or as bonsai.
The general principles for outdoor pruning apply, with the probable need to consider root pruning as well.

A well maintained camellia can be kept in its final container for many years without problem, with some root pruning carried out every five years or so. This means removing the plant from its container and probably finding a mass of densely packed, brown ineffective roots. The next step is to cut away several inches of root system from the root ball, the amount depending on the size of the root system, but about five to ten centimetres is usual. The plant is then replaced in its pot with new compost around the edge.
If this is not done periodically and the camellia appears to be out of control, too large, or looks poor despite all care, the easiest solution is for someone to take it off your hands and plant it out in a garden somewhere, having first made sure that a smaller plant is coming along as a replacement if it is a particular favourite. The very bold might like to try a rather more drastic measure as an alternative. This is to remove the whole plant from its container, then to use a large, sharp, knife to cut away 50% of the now densely matted root system. The camellia is then

repotted in its original container with fresh compost as above, watered well, and placed in a sheltered environment to recover. If the job is done in spring just as growth starts, the plant will soon get going again and rapidly produce a healthy young root system, with very little check to top growth. It is then left for a couple of years after which the other half of the root system is given the same treatment. Some people prune the top growth fairly hard to counteract the effect of losing so much root, and to stimulate new growth. Others get away with no pruning at all.

Choice of containers

If small, two or three-year-old camellias are purchased they will need to be potted on into pots of gradually increasing size, moving up from, say, two-litre after two years to four-litre and then eight or ten-litre size after another two, by which time the plants will probably be at least six years old. It is a mistake to pot up a small plant with a small root system straight into a large container, not only because it looks out of proportion, but because it is not good for the root systems of the plants. The proportion of compost is too great in relation to the roots and it tends to become sour, especially if water is abundant in it. This is because the root hairs are only able to take up moisture from the area around them, creating movement within that area, pulling more water in from only a small distance away, and at the same time encouraging air movement too.

Further away, there is no movement and a stagnant, airless atmosphere develops, unsuitable for the growing roots to penetrate into so they tend to rot before they have a chance to develop, and of course the plant suffers as a result and either dies or takes a very long time to recover. Once camellias reach the size where they look in balance with the chosen ornamental pot they can be moved up into it with confidence. If it is to remain in position on a particular site a 60cm or even larger container may be used, but this, with compost and plant added, is too large to move comfortably, so a smaller container will need to be chosen if the more mobile system of different summer and winter situations is to be used. It is quite possible to keep a camellia in a 30cm container for 12 years or more, but it is likely to look a little incongruous if allowed to grow naturally.

Apart from selecting the size and design of the final, ornamental containers, the material used has to be chosen to suit the site and personal preferences of the owners.

There is a variety of ornamental containers available: plastic, concrete, wood, glazed pottery, terracotta. Plastic tubs are available in a variety of shapes and colours, as well as sizes, with white being popular because it is designed to reflect the suns rays and reduce the risk of overheated roots. Some are almost identical to terra cotta at first glance, but very much cheaper. They tend to be light in weight, so some ballast in the form of non-calcareous stones or bricks may be useful, especially if a tall plant is likely to add to the instability. Concrete, or pseudo-stone has its advantages, with stability being the most obvious one. The acidity of an ericaceous compost, however, has sometimes been blamed for dissolving the cement in the concrete, releasing excess lime from cheaper containers of this type. A plastic lining solves the problem, but remember to puncture holes in it for drainage.

Wood is popular as a material for displaying camellias as it is good as an insulating material and will help prevent either overheating or chilling of roots. It can also be very pleasing to the eye, and harmonious with surroundings.

Wooden half barrels, or purpose made wooden 'Versailles' containers are for very large plants if they are to be kept in one place. Purchased wooden tubs and troughs are almost invariably ready for planting and need no further treatment, except possibly to enlarge the drainage holes. A keen handiman will make his/her own, using good quality wood, to whatever size and design fits the situation. Two things need to be borne in mind; one is the need to preserve the wood, as untreated wood will rot, and the second is that many wood preservatives give off fumes which can be harmful to plants. Particular attention needs to be given to the treatment of the inside of containers as the acidic nature of the compost, together with the chemical fertilizers in it, will rot wood very quickly. A good wood preservative selected as being safe for plants should be used well in advance of planting, and the containers left outdoors until no smell can be detected.

A plastic lining for the vertical sides can also be used as an additional barrier if it gives peace of mind. The outside of wooden containers can be treated with the same wood preservative, or painted green or some other colour which does not detract from the camellia foliage or flowers. Varnish is also used as an alternative to paint. The main thing is to construct and carry out all preserving and painting well in advance of potting.

The glazed pots, mostly supplied from China, are cheap and cheerful, with their dragon and other oriental designs, and are available in a variety of sizes. Terracotta, whether large or small, is the traditional material for pots, and there are many different designs to choose from, enough to suit all tastes. The more ornamental ones, however, may detract from the camellias they are supposed to display. Terracotta does tend to shatter with the freeze/thaw process in winter, but the chemical treatment designed to make them frost-proof seems to be effective in all but the most severe winters.

Drainage

Pot drainage is not a major problem in low rainfall areas, and most of the clay or terracotta pots seem to come from countries of low rainfall. They are often manufactured with drainage holes which are either too few or too small to provide efficient drainage where rainfall is more frequent and persistent. These holes should, if necessary, be enlarged by the careful use of a drill with a sharp masonry bit.

Large pots may need a layer of crocks or non-calcareous stones at the bottom to encourage efficient drainage, and it is often a good idea to raise pots off the ground on bricks or blocks of wood.

Compost needs to allow good drainage but must also be sufficiently water retentive to avoid the need for over frequent watering in summer. The ideal compost therefore consists of a mixture of both inorganic material, and organic matter. The inorganic or mineral material should be of a suitable size to encourage good aeration and drainage. Coarse sand or fine grit are good because they are also heavy enough to act as ballast for stability. Loam soil with a high percentage of clay particles can become compacted, dense and impenetrable for both roots and even water if dried out at any stage. Organic matter such as peat absorbs water like a sponge, and releases it gradually to the roots as they need it, but it can be too fine and even in texture and, if compressed, it forms a dense airless mass with poor drainage, which is unhealthy for roots. A mixture of coarse peat and well composted bark is an ideal organic blend because the bark provides a healthy mixture of textures.

Choice of compost

Acidity. There are many ericaceous composts on the market, which are specifically formulated for lime hating plants such as camellias, and most are peat based, with an index when sold of pH4 to 4.9, which is on the low side. This is fine in areas where water to be used for irrigation is alkaline because there is scope for a rise in pH, but it can cause problems after a year or two if water is neutral or acidic, as most camellias are not happy in levels below pH4.5.

It is not generally appreciated that camellias actually need a small amount of calcium, which in non-ericaceous composts is usually supplied by lime. However, composts which contain more than a trace of this should be avoided, as these will tip the balance too much towards alkalinity, which chemically locks up other essential minerals. Loam-based composts (eg, John Innes brands) often have an unacceptably high initial pH of 6.6 or above. They are difficult to assess as we do not generally know whether the source of the loam is an acidic or an alkaline soil, a predominantly clay or sand one, or even, as occasionally happens, one with viable weed seeds in it.

Most of the 'soil less' (ie, loam-free) composts based on peat which are sold as multi-purpose are acidic, around pH5 to pH5.8, and eminently suitable for camellias and other plants in the ericaceous category, even in areas where the irrigation water is alkaline, with a high pH (pH8 or more), and the kettle suffers from limescale. If there is a nagging worry, many people tend to use water which has passed through a water softener, which is not a good idea because the offending lime is replaced by sodium salts which are potentially even more damaging. It is better to neutralize the lime with a dose of acidifying ammonium sulphate. This also adds quickly available nitrogen salts. (One teaspoonful per gallon of water in early spring, repeated once, a month later, is recommended.) One of the specially formulated acidifying liquid fertilizers could be used as another alternative, following the instructions very carefully and measuring accurately. In these situations the use of an inexpensive pH kit is a great boon.

With the need to conserve peat supplies in some areas a number of other products have been tried as substitutes, including coir from coconut shells. Experiments have shown that camellias and rhododendrons do not thrive in it. However, shredded bark, in addition to helping aeration and drainage also acts as a chemical safety buffer for some of the fertilizers used. Camellias and other similar plants seem to do well.

Fertilizer for compost

The subject of the addition of chemical fertilizers to composts is a complex one; there are almost as many recipes as there are for fruit cake. Most camellias purchased from a nursery or garden centre will almost certainly have slow release fertilizer pellets included in their compost. They may look a little like slugs eggs, or they may be coloured blue or some other bright colour.

Each pellet consists of a polymer coating surrounding a carefully balanced compound fertilizer. The principle is that the polymer coating dissolves over a period of time, gradually releasing the fertilizer into the compost and, since the polymer is designed to dissolve when temperatures are relatively high, the fertilizer is only released in the growing season when the plants require it. In the early days there were problems with some of these products as excess fertilizer was released into compost in pots under glass during warm spells in mid-winter and many plants died as a result

of chemical root scorch. Now the scientists have perfected the product to the extent that not only has this problem been overcome, but formulations are available specifically for spring or autumn potting, and for release over a variety of periods of time. The only danger is in using compost which has been stored in a warm place, in which case there may be an accumulation of released fertilizer, which will need to be flushed out. This is easily done by flushing plenty of clean water through the compost immediately after potting.

Slow release pellets may be incorporated into home made mixes if desired, following the instructions which are supplied on the packet with care, of course.

Extra ingredients are sometimes used in potting mixes. Keiserite or magnesium limestone may be added as an alternative to lime in calcium form, not only to counteract excessive acidity, but also to supply magnesium as an essential mineral. A small amount of ammonium nitrate may be added as a source of additional nitrogen whcih will assist the bacteria necessary to rot down bark and peat.

One other, optional ingredient is silica gel. There are many versions available and they can be very useful in situations where compost dries out fast and the task of watering becomes a chore. They are chemically inactive but have the effect of reducing water loss by evaporation.

Recipe for camellia compost

Measurements are given by percentage. Volume is usually used as weights vary, depending on how wet the peat, bark and grit are. One method is to construct a box of one cubic metre and to mark on it the levels to give the required percentages of the first three ingredients. Tip out onto a suitably clean, dry surface. Then measure out the chemicals and mix the whole lot thoroughly.

> 75% coarse sphagnum moss peat (or 60% moss peat)
> 18% 1cm grade horticultural bark (or 15% sterilised loam)
> 7% coarse grit (non calcareous).
> **Add:**
> 1.8kg /cubic metre magnesium limestone
> 180gm/cu. metre ammonium nitrate
> 2 to 3kg/cu metre Osmocote slow release fertilizer.

Osmocote is the trade name of the slow-release fertilizer products most widely available worldwide. There are many others: Nutricote, Plantcote and Multicote are some of them. They vary as far as the duration of release is concerned, from three to four months to 12-14 months. They are designed to supply all the fertilizer needs of the plants for the duration stated.

The Osmocote formulation which acts over 12 to 14 months is most often used, so that if potting at the normal time, late spring or summer, there will be sufficient nutrient in the compost to last for one whole growing season plus the beginning of the next. Certainly no additional fertilizer should be given in the first year. When purchasing plants it is probably worth checking for the presence of slow release fertilizers in the compost. If the plant has been recently potted and/or pellets are found which have plenty of fertilizer in them when squashed, then care should be taken not to over feed in the first season if at all. It is rare to find pellets which have become completely drained of fertilizer so this has to be a matter of judgement.

If the above compost mix is not possible or acceptable, then the general principles of providing a foundation mixture of organic and inorganic materials, plus fertilizers, should be followed, but perhaps organically produced fertilizers used instead of the chemicals recommended, and peat substitutes used instead of peat. Well rotted leaf mould, especially that collected from under pine trees is excellent and there are some good organic fertilizers based on seaweed available in most countries.

Planting in containers

The same principles apply as when planting in the ground, with minor alterations.

Most modern camellia composts will not need to have broken crocks or stones put in the bottom of containers to encourage good drainage, and if necessary a piece of porous fabric can be placed across the larger drainage holes to stop compost falling through the larger holes. By the time this rots the compost will have settled.

Having assembled camellias, compost and containers, all is ready to plant up.

As with planting in the garden, it is important to check the camellias first to make sure the roots are healthy, to tease them out if pot bound and too closely packed, to cut back any tap root encircling the root ball, and to have a good look for predators such as vine weevil grubs. Check that the compost is damp.

It is then time to put sufficient compost in the pot for the plant to sit on, place the root ball in the centre of the pot, and fill in with more compost. Modern composts should not be rammed in, but should be gently firmed and the pot shaken to ensure there are no air pockets. The end result should be a camellia with compost surrounding the root ball, but not covering it, and there should be enough room at the top of the pot to allow for watering, but not too much room as the compost shrinks as it rots. The same problem arises with camellias potted too deep as garden plants; they are very likely to die as a result of bark rot.

Having finished planting, the camellia should be very thoroughly watered until water runs out of the bottom of the pots, and then be allowed to settle.

After-care of container-grown camellias

Because they are grown in a restricted way, container-grown camellias need more care than garden grown ones, particularly with regard to watering. Feeding is also essential as these plants are not able to spread their roots in search of naturally available nutrients. Pruning is also necessary to keep shapes under control.

Watering

This is no problem for the experienced gardener who soon gets to know the requirements of his/her plants, but it is one of the biggest sources of uncertainty for the newer enthusiast.
A large rainwater tank is ideal, but mains water is fine. If this is alkaline an acidifying liquid feed will be useful to counteract possible over alkaline conditions, but must be used with great care. Water should be supplied when the soil starts to dry out and before the compost gets dehydrated completely; it is difficult to re-hydrate a peat-based compost, apart from the likely damage to a wilting plant. It is better to soak the compost thoroughly and then leave well alone for several days, or more, than to give water little and often, as the latter method rarely allows the water to penetrate to the bottom of the root system and there is often moisture only in the top layer of compost, with dangerously dry compost underneath. There are water checking probes available for those who require them.

Feeding

This subject is dealt with in more detail under the heading of 'Soil fertility and nutrients'. Liquid feeding is favoured for supplying nutrients in areas where water is required frequently during the growing season, especially where accurate control is required and the camellia collection is small, whereas a top dressing of granular fertilizer is often used when there are many plants and accurate control is not deemed essential. Camellias are very flexible and, provided they are not overfed, they will usually continue to thrive whatever method is chosen. It is essential to follow the instructions on the bottle or packet, and to underfeed rather than overdo it. Also, bear in mind the size and vigour of the plants, giving small plants much less than mature ones and vigorous varieties more than slow growing ones. It does not take long to get to know them and their needs.

Containers under glass or other full protection

Where there is plenty of space camellias may be grown in borders, planted directly into the ground in a glasshouse or polythene tunnel. However, many people prefer to grow in containers as it is more flexible.

Growing under full protection is a system which camellia enthusiasts may choose in the cooler climates, where the need for frost protection is greater and the need to give extra encouragement to flower bud formation may be critical. It enables collectors, especially those who seek the rare and/or tender to enlarge the range collected, and it allows exhibitors in all areas to grow high quality blooms, undamaged by the elements, particularly the white and pale pink varieties or those with extra large blooms or poor petal texture which show such damage more readily. Scented species and cultivars can also be appreciated more in the warm, still air of a glasshouse.

When camellias in containers are kept entirely under the protection of a cold glasshouse, conservatory or plastic tunnel, the environment for the whole year needs to be considered, together with the needs of any other plants which are to be grown. If using a conservatory attached to a home, owners are likely to use it as an extra room, in which case human comfort may have to be considered before the needs of the plants. Most camellias prefer to avoid extremes of temperature and humidity just as we do, although, like us, they can usually cope with them if they have to for brief periods, but may suffer and not give of their best if they continue for too long. Camellias do not like a hot dry atmosphere in winter; the sort of atmosphere we provide for ourselves in our modern, centrally heated homes. In winter they should be kept in an environment which is cool and well ventilated, as good air circulation reduces the risk of fungal diseases which can spoil both flowers and leaves. It also reduces the risk of flower bud drop which can cause such disappointment.

In cold climates, flowering will tend to be several weeks earlier than outside, and, in the warm environment of a glasshouse the flowering season is likely to be shorter; everything is speeded up and more comparable with outdoor growing in warm climates, including flower forms, with varieties such as C. x *williamsii* 'Dream Boat', or C. *japonica* 'Desire', which have formal double flowers outside in cold climates, probably having a 'rosebud' or 'bullnose' centre.

Large blooms are produced under the protection of this small glasshouse

A home-made conservatory makes it possible to enjoy camellias in a hostile climate

GROWING UNDER GLASS

Choice of glasshouse and its equipment
The size of the glasshouse will be decided
according to individual circumstances, and its site
may well be restricted to what is available. Ideally it
should be in a situation where it gets good light in
winter but some shade in the height of the day in
summer, and should be big enough to allow for an
enthusiasm which can become addictive.
There should be plenty of height to allow for future
growth, and it should be high sided so that tall
varieties can be put behind smaller ones on either
side of a central path. The pitch should be such
that drips from condensation do not spoil blooms.

It is useful to have a partition so that one end
may be kept separate for propagation, or any other
activities which need a different environment from
the main area. Benching may be useful here.

Flooring

Concrete or stone paving slabs are probably the
favoured floor types as they are easy to keep clean
and some drainage is possible between them.
Solid concrete is even more hygienic, while small
washed gravel gives both drainage and is
aesthetically pleasing, although it is not as easy to
maintain hygiene.

Extras

Electricity supplied to the glass house enables the
owner to have light for carrying out intricate
tasks such as grafting on dull days, and enables
him/her to have soil warming and a mist unit for
propagation. Electricity may be needed for space
heating if this is supplied by an electrical heater,
or an electrically operated thermostat may be
used to control other forms of heating. The main
aim is to prevent frost damaging roots so the
thermostat needs to be set to provide warmth
when the temperature drops to about 5°C. For

The collection lives inside in winter, but outside in a shade house in summer

those who like things to be automatic it also allows for certain types of automatic ventilators; these can be controlled to close when the temperature drops to 8°C and to open by degrees from that point upwards so that there is full ventilation at 17°C and above in both winter and summer. The cubic capacity of the glasshouse will have to be calculated before buying a heater in order to get one which will give the correct output.

Water needs to be available, preferably both from the mains and from a stored supply of rainwater in a nearby tank or water butt. The latter is important if the mains supply is alkaline, with the mains being used when the rain water runs out. A tap with a hose to which a lance may be fitted, is useful, to give a spray if required. It is also possible to have a system for trickle or drip irrigation to individual containers, and, for those people who are likely to be away a lot, it is possible to get a completely automatic system.

General management under glass
Autumn/winter
Camellias should be kept on the dry side during the winter months although there will be a need for occasional watering, especially during warm spells when the temperature may rise sufficiently for evaporation to take place. As with any camellias, feeding should be avoided throughout the dormant, winter season.

When any frost is forecast all vents should be closed several hours before sunset to conserve warmth and to stop air circulation, or at least reduce it to a minimum. It is a fact, that if the compost does freeze through for a few days, there is less likely to be damage in an environment with still air than one where air is moving because the wind chill factor is significantly damaging.

Spring and summer
During the main spring flowering season there is little to be done to the camellias except to enjoy

them, and to dead-head those varieties which are not self-grooming. Soil should be kept moist, and it will be noticed that water is in progressively more demand as roots start to grow and become more active.

Feeding should start as soon as signs of growth are becoming evident, and follow the same procedure as with other camellias, with perhaps greater consideration being given to liquid feeding, especially if this is used on other plants in the same area. For those who prefer to do so, a top dressing of a suitable granular fertilizer may be used.

Attention to hygiene is needed in order to keep pests and diseases at bay. Predators of insect pests do not usually have the same access to them as they do in a garden, and fungal spores thrive under glass. Dead flowers should be regularly removed from the floor and, if necessary, from the plants, especially in areas where flower blight is a problem. Any diseased or damaged shoots should be promptly removed and all prunings burned.

Pruning

Growth under glass is more vigorous and early, and the need to maintain shape becomes more relevant, especially in a small area, so pruning becomes very important. The accent is even sometimes on regular pinching out during the growing season, rather than relying on a secateur job to take out bigger growth after flowering, if young plants are to be encouraged to be bushy. It is important to get the right balance as over-dense bushes may suffer from fungal die-back in the centre caused by lack of air circulation. This is more of a problem in climates which are warm in winter.

Shading

Early growth is one of the main advantages of protected growing as it means that vegetative growth is mature in time for flower buds to be given more chance to form. However, young growth is tender and even more vulnerable under glass, so shading should be supplied early, before there is any risk of scorch. Blinds of various materials are available, or white glasshouse shade paint may be sprayed over the outside of the glass. It may need topping up if heavy rain is experienced before the end of summer.

During extra hot weather, when it feels uncomfortable to walk into the glasshouse, it is a good idea to spray over the camellias with cool water, making sure that any hot water that has accumulated in the pipes is run off first, of course. Cool water is not likely to scorch the leaves if they are adequately shaded.

CAMELLIA BEDS

This system is ideal for those who have unsuitable soil or none at all, or those who are unable to cope with the regular watering which pots and tubs require. It is an excellent compromise between the natural and the artificial, and can add an exciting ornamental feature, especially to a courtyard or other enclosed area, where beds can be created against walls or freely designed to various shapes in the middle.

The surface area of the bed obviously depends on individual circumstances, as does the depth to a certain extent, but sufficient depth should be allowed for roots to not only form anchors to prevent the camellias blowing over later, but also to allow them to spread downwards, below the risk of frost in cold areas, and into cool, moist soil in hot seasons. A root system with room to spread will, of course, be more efficient at absorbing both water and nutrients than a small restricted one. Provision needs to be made for drainage of excess water as well, especially in the smaller beds in small areas.

Retaining walls may be of bricks or similar materials, well weathered, or of treated wood, or peat blocks and the bed should be partially sunk below soil level, at least to the depths of the foundations of the wall, lower if construction is in soil which is not excessively alkaline (over pH8). A plastic or other non-porous material should be used as a liner to prevent alkaline water seeping into the bed. Some people sit this on a 5cm layer of non-calcareous sand, which may have further foundations below to encourage drainage. It helps the plastic liner to sit snugly without being pierced in unwanted areas by underlying stones.

The wall is then built so that the final depth of the bed is at least 60cm, preferably more.

Holes are punctured in the base of the lining to ensure that excess water escapes.

Coarse gravel, to a depth of 10cm may be used at the bottom, but there is debate about the effectiveness of this as some feel that it does not help to encourage drainage.

Lastly, a suitable general purpose compost, or an ericaceous mix, is used to fill the bed, and it is firmed down to make it ready for a final raking to level it before planting up in the usual way.

The choice of camellias for beds is obviously a personal one, and depends also on the size of beds. It is possible to choose camellia varieties to flower in all seasons except summer, and the careful choice of companion plants which should include other shrubs, herbaceous plants, corms and bulbs, which enjoy the same conditions, will give year-round interest at all levels.

Camellias and cherry blossom

4

Using Camellias In The Garden

Camellias have be thought of as among the most versatile and useful plants in the garden, with their generally glossy, always evergreen leaves and their tremendous range of habits, leaf shape and size, and their variety of flower form, size, colour and season. They are probably best grown as dominant plants for their flowering season, fading into a background role to give prominance to other plants for the rest of the year. With their relative freedom from pests and diseases and undemanding cultural requirements they can certainly be considered low maintenance plants. They lend themselves to a variety of garden designs in small, medium or large gardens and to planting in public places such as parks, roadside verges and as city centre features outside prominent buildings.

Camellias are regarded as high value, permanent, rather than temporary, plants, and as such it pays to give some thought to their purchase and siting. Each person will have different ideas about what he/she requires of

them, and much will depend on what the site has in terms of size, soil, aspect and space, not to mention existing plants. A general overview is therefore first needed. Are camellias to give maximum effect, perhaps to hit the eye with a bold splash of colour? Or is it the intention to create interest by more subtle means, by planting varieties which are unusual and somehow different as individual plants, the sort which make people pause and look more closely? If the latter, beware – the owners are highly likely to become collectors!

English gardens are probably more landscaped than those in other countries, with more thought given to both the overall artistic effect and to detail. For smaller, suburban homes in particular, the garden becomes an extension of the house; an expression of the personality of the owners, and camellias can be very expressive in this way, with scope to make quite definite statements by using particular colours, for example. An all-white garden is popular in inner city gardens with camellia varieties such as 'Lovelight' used as features, where there is plenty of shelter, but perhaps little sun or space; a haven of tranquility for a busy executive. Generally speaking, the smaller the garden the more the accent is on individual flowers which are best appreciated close up, so varieties with big blooms are often chosen, while varieties which carry a mass of smaller flowers have more effect in larger gardens where they are more likely to be seen from a distance. Whatever the situation, there is a need to anticipate the future because each camellia will grow in its own way, and will reach its ultimate dimensions in due course, so it is useful to have some idea what to expect. It is also worth considering whether to control shape and size by pruning as the plants develop, or whether it is possible to allow sufficient space for natural development in the first place. A good specialist nursery supplier should be able to give general information about each variety sold, but will not be able to be absolutely specific, as much will depend on the individual soil conditions and micro-climate of the garden. What should be avoided at all costs is the planting of a vigorous variety in a small space, followed by years of unchecked growth, until the camellia becomes an undesirable liability instead of a pleasure. It will then either have to be removed, have its top taken out, or it will need to be 'hat racked' or even sawn almost to ground level and allowed to start again in order to be grown in future in a more controlled manner.

PLANNING A CAMELLIA BORDER

The assumption is that the camellias are to be the dominant feature in their flowering season, but will become background plants at other times to allow other plants to take over as the main focus of attention during the year. The choice of other plants will be a matter of personal choice and may be permanent plantings, or of a seasonal, temporary, nature. If the latter, the shallow feeding roots of the camellias will have to be watched to avoid too much disturbance to them when cultivating the soil for these subjects.

It is normal to plant camellias in groups, especially in larger gardens, to give interest in terms of colour and flowering season over a period of up to six months. They can then be given the same mulch, feed and water together, which makes life easier. Where there is plenty of space the groups can be of three or more of the same variety to make more of an impression.

Much will depend on the size of the border, but the same general principles apply whatever the size; it is just a matter of scaling up or down. The following is intended for the smaller suburban or semi-suburban garden as a start.

Camellias, as the dominant backbone of the border, will need to be chosen first in the initial design. There is no need to stick to the 'tallest at the back' and 'shortest at the front' principle; it may create more interest to mix them, but it is certainly a good idea to use slopes and banks to good advantage by choosing low growing or cascading varieties to show themselves at their best at the bottom of the slope, while tall varieties which carry their blooms in a pendant manner can be planted so that the blooms can be best seen from below. Rounded, bushy, moderately fast growing cultivars, or those with a spreading habit can fill in the space between. If there is no slope, tall varieties can be used to give height to the centre of an island border, or the back of a boundary one. The less vigorous are useful to fill in between others at the back, and in the rest of the border, with one or two taller ones carefully used among them to form bays, with either low or slow growing varieties filling the

It is useful to anticipate the eventual size and shape of camellias

space between. Other plants may be used to give contrast and seasonal variation. It is generally best to allow each to be accessible enough to take a closer look at the blooms and, if used, to read the labels, without trampling on foreground plants, so the border should not be too wide. Most gardeners plant far too closely and need to either thin out later, or prune annually to keep the camellias far enough apart to retain the individuality of each. This will be apparent after four or five years which will not be too late to lift and move plants.

COMPANION PLANTS
PERMANENT PLANTINGS
Winter interest

Shrubs: Witch hazel (*Hamamellis mollis cvs*) and Mahonia species and their cultivars, are both available in scented forms. The coloured winter

stems of some of the Salix are very attractive too. In the foreground, maybe some winter flowering heathers such as *E. carnea* 'Springwood White', planted in blocks of at least seven.

Spring interest

Plants for this period will need to contrast with or complement the flowers of the camellias. There is a vast number to choose from, so only a small number is suggested here. They should not be too showy or they will lead the eye away from the glory of the camellias, nor should they have flowers which clash too starkly with the colours of the camellia varieties nearby. To both give contrast and to enhance: *Amelanchier* and some of the dainty, small-flowered *Prunus* or *Malus* are useful. Later, the white racemes of the many species and cultivars of *Pieris*, followed by the varying reds of the young growth, tend to take over as the majority of the camellias pass their peak. Some space should surely be found for one or more magnolias; perhaps the beautiful waxy white, scented flowered *M. x loebneri* 'Merrill', or *M. stellata*, or one of its forms, all of which are slow growing and compact and suitable for small gardens. Larger gardens can accomodate the more vigorous *M. soulangeana* and its hybrids. Bulbs, especially *Narcissus*, are obvious choices for foreground effect. Other, slightly more unusual plants which look wonderful in the foreground are the *Erythronium*s (dogs tooth violets), both the yellow *E. tuolumnense* or the cultivar 'Pagoda', and the beautiful pink *E. revolutum* 'johnsonii'are worth the trouble which may need to be taken to acquire the tubers, or young plants. They enjoy the shelter and shade given by more mature camellias and the richly organic soil under them and, with their attractive leaves and proudly held flowers, never fail to give an unusual and attractive effect.

In late spring the evergreen azaleas, now classified as rhododendrons, provide an excellent foil to the last few camellia flowers, and their bright colours soon take over as a prominent display in their own right. They are often planted en masse, and, provided the varieties are chosen carefully, may give a flowering season of up to eight weeks, and a good range of sizes and habits, with colours which are often very bright and look good against the dark green foliage of the camellias. In warmer climates such as the southern States of the USA, South Africa, and most of Australia and New Zealand the *indica* azaleas will thrive, but these are not hardy enough for the colder regions of the USA, northern Europe and the UK. Here the hardier Kaempferi, Kurume, or Glenn Dale azaleas will give good value, with some of the ground-hugging Nakaharae or North Tisbury varieties used as border-edge plants.

Summer interest

The evergreen azaleas take the border into mid-summer, which is often a rather blank time for shrubs in a mixed permanent border. Bulbs such as lilies look good, especially if they are planted amongst the azaleas, which support their often fragile stems. The attractive leaves of so many hostas contrast well with the dark green camellias and the red-hued leaves and deep red flowers of *Lobelia cardinalis* add more contrast. Later the cold climate loving *Mecanopsis*, which enjoy the semi-shade provided by camellias, can be planted in groups towards the back of the border in gaps between groups of camellias. The bright blue of *M. betonicifolia* or the yellow of *M. chelidonifolia* have an air of character and surprise about them and both set seed relatively freely.

Year-round interest

Where low maintenance is really important and diversity is not a pre-requisite, ground cover plants such as a selection of ivies (*Hedera*) particularly the variegated ones, or simply the old favourite *Vincas*, *major* or *minor*, will soon cover the foreground and help to stifle the weeds.

Temporary plantings

Provided that damage to the surface roots of camellias can be avoided, some very effective displays can be created by using short season bedding schemes, particularly in smaller gardens or more formal areas in public parks where colour is expected for most of the year. There is something very enriching about a massed planting of large, gaudy, tuberous-rooted begonias in front of the dark green of a massed planting of camellias. Dahlias give a similar show in late summer and early autumn.

Camellias as feature plants

Sometimes a single camellia of particularly interesting form or habit can be used as a feature plant; for example the narrow, almost fastigiate hybrid 'Spring Festival' is outstanding as a camellia to provide contrasting height in a heather border or rockery. It produces a profusion of flowers, which last for up to six weeks, in all but the coldest areas, and has attractive bronze young growth in late spring and in late summer. It is happy in full sun or semi-shade, but will not always flower well in full shade in colder areas. Other taller but slightly wider growers make excellent focal points for a vista. The pale pink flowers of a single plant of 'Charles Colbert' or even paler 'Felice Harris', covering almost every centimetre of the bush, can look stunning in a cool, shady, even dark site.

Similarly, a well chosen camellia looks marvellous planted in a lawn, or two or three well-spaced plants grown as individual features in grass under the dappled shade of cherry trees.

If care of a natural garden is difficult, for instance, if the owner is disabled, then spaces can be left in paved areas for camellias of particular merit. They should be self-grooming varieties so they look good throughout the flowering season without the bother of removing spent blooms from the bushes. Upright varieties such as 'Inspiration' or 'Donation' are good choices.

Cascading varieties like 'Taro-an', or if in a mild climate, 'Quintessence' or 'Sweet Emily Kate', may be used to feature on either side of the top or bottom of a flight of steps. The last two varieties are scented so they give an added bonus, but are not hardy enough outside in cold climates. In a similar situation, or in a formal garden, or at a focal point where formality may be effective, one or a pair of very slow growing bushes kept to a round or conical shape look

'Donation', pruned carefully and regularly, makes an excellent feature shrub in a paved area

'Leonard Messel' flowers mid to late season and looks well with Pieris

good. *C. japonica* 'Hassaku' is suitable for any climate, *C.* x *williamsii* 'Contribution' in a cold area, and the dwarf *C. sasanquas* such as 'Paradise Little Liane', 'Paradise Petite' or 'Tanya' in a hot situation.

In all cases where camellias are being used as

'Donation, left to its own devices will grow into a big, bold bush

The Camellia Walk at Leonardslee Gardens in Sussex, England, allows plent of space for camellias to grow fairly naturally

feature plants the growth habit is of great significance when selecting varieties and choosing plants, but the flowering habit is, of course, important too. Where feature plants are seen at a distance, as in the case of 'Spring Festival' in a large heather garden, the individual blooms are not as important as the general effect. The blooms on camellias which are to be seen at close quarters take on more significance and can certainly add interest or even drama to an otherwise dull area. The tiered growth habit of varieties such as 'Apollo', 'Grand Slam' or 'Guilio

Established camellias in
the background awaiting
foreground planting

Tulips with late blooming
camellias in Nantes,
France

Nuccio' make these ideal varieties to put on a
corner site where such plants catch the eye from
several angles, and each has attractive flowers
which have character as individuals, to be enjoyed
both from a distance and at close quarters. Few
camellia enthusiasts can be without *C. x
williamsii* 'Jury's Yellow' or the similar
'Brushfields Yellow' or 'Gwenneth Morey', and

these, because they are 'different' and rather
special, can be given a special spot. They do need
shelter and can be fussy until the right place is
found for them. In a small garden it might be
necessary to concentrate on small growing, small
or miniature-flowered varieties, and one of the
more spectacular of these can be used as a special
feature. The very free flowering, slow growing

Daffodils and camellias
go well together

Camellias growing happily beside a mangrove swamp in New Zealand

The bright flowers of 'Debbie' are difficult to tone with,
but this azalea does not clash

Left: Camellias beside the sea at Porthpean near St Austell
in Cornwall

'Adolphe Audusson' with well chosen pansies in the foreground

'Adolphe Audusson' at the front door

hybrid 'Nicky Crisp' may have simple flowers, but they have a special clarity about them and are produced in profusion over a long period. They also fall whole to the ground when spent so the bush always looks tidy.

Camellias for hedging

Evergreen hedges which do not produce flowers of any significance have their place, but once a camellia hedge has been seen in its flowering season it will not be forgotten. Even amongst the upright growing varieties, which are obviously the most suitable for the taller hedges, there are so many different rates of growth, so there are many situations in which camellias may be used, but it is desirable to choose varieties with a similar rate of growth for each hedge. All can be pruned or clipped and shaped after each flush of growth, as with any other evergreen hedge, but late clipping which might stimulate growth too late to ripen before winter frosts, should be avoided in cold climate areas.

'Donation' enhances the white walls of this bungalow but is in danger of getting out of control

The cheerful flowers of this low growing camellia hedge brighten up the greyness of a street in Cornwall

Informal hedging

This may be more accurately described as screening because this is where upright varieties of moderately dense habit are used to perhaps hide an ugly feature, divide a garden into two areas, or even to give a more interesting facing or added height to a boundary wall or fence.

The hedge may be of a single variety or of a selection of different ones, in which case varieties of similar habit and speed of growth should be chosen. For quick results choose rapid growers such as 'Debbie', 'Inspiration', or 'St Ewe' in colder climates, and autumn flowering cultivars of *C. sasanqua* such as 'Hugh Evans', 'Nodami-ushiro' or the newer 'Paradise Venessa' in areas where there is plenty of sun and warmth in summer. All will stand full sun. Plant about 60cm apart and they will draw each other up as they grow, needing little attention apart from the removal of the odd wayward branch, a little water and feed in the early years, and possibly a spray with insecticide if necessary.

Formal hedging

For less rapid growth and a denser hedge, the hybrids 'Anticipation', 'Ballet Queen' and 'Tiptoe' are ideal in cooler climates, as they all grow into bushy plants naturally, needing little or no pruning or clipping, but all three appreciate some shade from the mid-day sun to avoid spoilt leaves and blooms. *C. japonica* varieties which make good naturally grown hedges include 'Alexander Hunter', 'Commander Mulroy', 'Janet Waterhouse' and 'Lady Loch'. They will need virtually no pruning except to decide on the ultimate height required, when any leading shoot may have to be removed.

For a really tightly controlled formal hedge, the small leaves and dense habit of some of the *C. sasanqua* varieties make very attractive, easily clippable hedges, particularly in most of Australia and other areas where full, hot sun is the summer norm and their autumn flowers make them even

A camellia hedge forming a spectacular boundary to a property in New Zealand

more appreciated than their spring flowering
relatives. Even without flowers, their foliage is
highly attractive, but most have small, single or
semi-double flowers which are not easily
squashed by the dense foliage of a moderately
clipped hedge, so they give a good show over a six
to ten-week period in autumn. Older *sasanqua*
varieties to include 'Mignonne', 'Navajo',
'Yuletide', and the newer Paradise series: Paradise
'Little Liane' and 'Paradise Petite', and for a
really dwarf hedge on a par with the low box
(*Buxus*) so widely used in knot gardens.

Planting and care of a camellia hedge

Even for an informal hedge it is desirable to plant
the camellias much more closely than normal –
about 60cm is fine for the larger informal or formal
hedging varieties. The dwarf hedgers need to be no
more than 30cm apart. Plants of similar vigour and
even quality should be chosen, either all of the
same variety or of different but compatible varieties
if a range of colours, flowering season and/or leaf
type is wanted. It is a matter of personal choice.
Ground preparation and actual planting are the
same as for any camellia.

It is useful to have a vision of the ultimate
dimensions of the newly planted hedge at the
outset, so that it can be allowed to develop as
naturally as possible, but controlled if necessary
by pruning or clipping young growth before it
hardens and becomes woody. So many people are
reluctant to take the secateurs or shears to
camellias, but the bushes respond so well to
snipping and shearing that there need be no
hesitation. There should be sufficient ripened
growth left to allow flower buds to develop on the
shorter shoots remaining.

With camellias of naturally dense habit
growing closely together extra concentration may
be needed to reach the inner parts of the hedge

with insecticide or fungicide sprays, if they are
required.
Suggested situations for hedges include:
Boundary hedge around a property – much more
interesting than laurel or privet.
Boundary around a feature or to make a
compartment within a garden – this might be to
separate the vegetable garden from the
ornamental, or to create a 'secret' garden area
within an ornamental garden.

Outlines for small formal beds. Dwarf
varieties are ideal to create outlines for formal
beds which may be used for seasonal bedding or
for herbs, etc. If the flowering season for the
camellias does not coincide with the peak season
for the bedding so much the better. The autumn
flowering *C. sasanqua*s fit in well here.

Camellias for special purposes

The growth habit of some varieties can be used to
create plants which can be trained for purposes to
suit individual sites and owners.

Semi-standards and standards

Although usually grown in containers there are
plenty of situations where camellias trained as
standards can be used in the garden, for
example as feature plants in a formal border in
a lawn, or one on either side of an entrance or
pathway. Semi-standards, being lower in height
than standards, will be good for smaller scale
situations. The key to creating such a formal
and unnatural plant is to choose one which has
produced a single strong stem which can be kept
going as a 'leader' until the desired height has
almost been reached. Alternatively a strong
growing variety can be chosen as a stock plant,
grown up to the required height as a standard,
and then the chosen variety grafted onto this.
Strong lateral stems should be removed as close

Espaliers need training on canes to start with

Some nurseries sell their less bushy camellias tied back onto trellises

to the single main stem and as tidily as possible, but still possibly leaving ugly-looking little stumps if the laterals are substantial. These will become less prominent in time. Small leafy shoots which will not leave too big a scar should be left in much the same way as maiden apple trees being trained as standards are feathered. This greenery will continue to manufacture sugars by photosynthesis and will help to build both the showy top of the standard and the strength of the stem. For the same reason, the top should not be fully shaped for a year or so after the main laterals have been removed from the stem, but the leading shoot, if there is one, can be cut back. A stake will probably be needed as support at least for the first few years.

Once the standard has been established as such, its top can be developed. This will depend on the variety chosen. *C. japonica* 'Tomorrow's Dawn' makes a very heavy standard with enormous flowers and large leaves. The versatile hybrid 'Spring Festival' is altogether more lightweight, in keeping with its much smaller neater but stiffly formal flowers, while varieties such as the scented hybrid 'Quintessence' can be allowed to cascade. Whatever the variety the training of the top is easy, just requiring the pinching out of young growth sufficient to keep the overall shape as the plant grows and once it has been established. It may be necessary to thin out the odd branch to prevent overcrowding and to allow the blooms to be well displayed.

Topiary

Small-leafed camellias such as many of the *sasanqua* varieties, can be the source of fun in the garden. By choosing one with a naturally dense habit, which can either be trained on its own roots or grafted onto another more vigorous grower, all sorts of shapes can be created, from low growing cocks and cats, or formal globes, to similar shapes grown higher as standards. Regular clipping and perhaps the internal staking and tying of the odd misplaced branch is all that is required, bearing in mind that branches can be positioned while they are green and flexible, and should remain in position once the wood hardens after a year or so. With very heavy pruning the foliage rather than the flowers will be of dominant interest.

(Hanging baskets and bonsai dealt with previously on separate pages.)

Camellias against walls and fences

How many shrubs will cover a wall, perhaps one in deep shade, and give a glorious display of flowers for several months either in autumn, winter or spring? There seems to be no end to the versatility of the camellia. There are varieties to grow to the height of a two-storey building, varieties to spread horizontally under the windows, and others to fit into odd narrow corners against buildings. Some are best left to grow naturally, with the odd trim to keep control, many can be trained as espaliers or fans more or less flat against any vertical surface. Others just need that extra protection to do well.

Free-growing camellias provide a foreground for a wall or fence and are particularly useful when the background needs regular treatment or painting as they can be relatively easily pulled forward and held away from the wall while work is done. An unattractive feature, say a drainpipe, can be disguised by an attractive camellia too. At the same time an attractive wall, especially a white, mellow brick or stone one, will give a good background to display camellia blooms to perfection and emphasise the glossy green leaves when not in flower. Almost any camellia looks

good, but brightly coloured bricks can create colour problems; it has been known for a customer to return a camellia which took hours to choose, 'because it clashed with my wall'! Most camellias will benefit from wall protection, but another angle to consider, particularly if wall/fence space is limited, is that some varieties may struggle for one reason or another as free standing plants out in a border, but will thrive when given the extra protection of a wall. The border may be too sunny, too windy, or too shady, or a combination of any two of these. With a choice of north, south, east or west aspects round a house, each giving its particular type of protection, there must surely be one which suits a fussy but highly desirable camellia.

C. reticulata cultivars and hybrids such as 'Captain Rawes' and 'Royalty' have good big, showy blooms in borders in most gardens in the far south west of England, but generally fail to flower regularly in gardens in most other areas of the country. Planted against a sheltered wall of almost any aspect, they will perform well in gardens up to the south of Scotland. Left to grow naturally these camellias have a more open habit than other camellias and will spread outwards from the wall too, so they can either be curbed just when really necessary or trained more closely to the desired shape against the wall. The *reticulata* hybrid 'Francie. L', with its characteristic, leathery, strap-shaped leaves which some find unattractive, will flower in most areas in the UK, but does even better against a wall. Its leaves are broader and even glossy given this shelter.

Many varieties of *C. japonica* which have white, pale pink, or large, thin textured flowers which damage easily, do better against a sheltering wall, protected from the prevailing wind and the fiercest mid-day sun, and *C.*

The success of 'Francie L' has encouraged this householder to plant more camellias against the tall boundary wall

Elegant camellias against the white walls of an elegant house in Cornwall

sasanqua varieties which enjoy more warmth and sun than other camellias can be persuaded to flower more freely in cooler climates when grown against a sunny south-facing wall or fence.

These then are the camellias which should have priority for limited wall space. A further dimension occurs here: provided the border adjacent to the wall is wide enough, why not train tall growing varieties such as 'Francie. L' flat against the wall, with free-standing camellias needing wall protection planted in the border 60 to 90cm in front of them, or at a smaller distance in between them? This brings out one more advantage of training against a wall or fence; it allows the owner to get more camellias into a small space.

Camellias as espaliers or fans

The choice of variety is the first step. Almost any camellia except the very bushy varieties will do, but full enjoyment depends on the aspect to a certain extent. In areas of high temperatures and light intensity at bud setting time in mid-summer any aspect will suit the *C. sasanqua* varieties, while some of the *C. japonica* cultivars will find the sunny aspects too sunny and will not only have scorched and damaged leaves, but damaged flowers as well. In colder areas where light intensity is also likely to be poor, the *williamsii* varieties are the only ones likely to succeed against a shady wall following an average summer. Ideally, varieties which grow long, whippy, flexible branches should be first choice as they are easier to place where you want them.

The next step is to decide on the ultimate dimensions required of the plants. Is the espalier or fan to be a low one, covering a wall below a window? Or is a tall growing variety required? A specialist nursery should be able to help with this selection of varieties and with the final choice of actual plants.

Some nurseries sell camellias already started on small wooden or plastic frameworks. Care should be taken when selecting from these as some are simply bushy, slow growing varieties which have turned out a bit leggy and are more easily sold on a frame, but may not be the best varieties for the job. Delve a little deeper and find out more about the true characteristics of each variety before buying.

Some preparation needs to be carried out before planting; trellis or wiring will be needed to tie the growing camellia branches back to. For the first six years growth this needs to be about 20cm apart for more slow growing varieties and 30cm for the vigorous *reticulata* ones like 'Francie L'. Planting technique is the same as for any camellia, but make sure that there is plenty of moisture-retentive organic matter in the soil as walls often cast rain shadows and borders beneath them are notorious for being dry. Also watch out for mortar rubble around the footings; the lime from this can cause alkalinity problems, so it should either be removed or heavy-duty plastic sheeting used to separate the planting area from the wall. It might even be worth removing all the soil from the border and replacing it with a compost of known acidity. Having planted the camellia it should be cared for in the normal way, with extra care being taken over supplying sufficient water, even in winter. Branches should be tied back into the desired positions as they grow, and those which are out of place removed, remembering that flowers will be produced on the mature young growth from earlier in the season.

BREEDING NEW CAMELLIAS

Camellia flowers are pollinated mainly by bees, with pollen from one flower being carried in the pollen sacs on their legs to the sticky, receptive stigma of another, with most of the transfer taking place between plants which are close to each other. In many of the wild camellia growing areas of southern China the flowering season is relatively dry, wild bees are active, and temperatures of 17 to 24°C frequently occur even in early spring. This is warm enough to activate pollen and also to make the ovules receptive in the ovaries below the stigma (15°C is the minimum). Once pollination, followed by fertilisation, has occurred, the seeds develop in the fruit and six or seven months later the fruit splits open to release the seeds onto the ground below. In the wild it is now autumn/early winter, and the climate cold and wet, so they remain, being chilled but moist, in the leaf litter under the seed parent bush until temperatures rise sufficiently for germination to take place in the spring.

Though there are over 32,000 named varieties of camellia in the *International Register*, it can be great fun to have a go at producing a few more! In Britain, northern Europe and much of the northern States of the USA it is often too cold for reliable pollination and fertilisation outdoors, but the warmer climates of most of Australia, South Africa, New Zealand and the southern and western States of the USA have higher temperatures at flowering time so pollination by the bees is more likely. Seeds are produced in abundance, and bushes can become quite loaded down with fruit, popularly known in New Zealand as 'apples'.

These seeds, can be harvested as soon as the first fruit splits. Some of the characteristics from the known parent will be transferred to the offspring so it pays to select seed from plants which have some particularly desirable feature which just might be carried forward to make that unique and highly unusual camellia – every camellia breeder's dream. It will take a minimum of three years in ideal conditions before one or more flowers are produced, but it just could be worth exhibiting, registering and marketing. Alternatively, it could be yet another red or pink single or semi-double with nothing special about it, or even one which fails to produce a flower for 14 years! Rejected seedlings make excellent stock plants for grafting, so the fun of the gamble is worth it anyway.

Even in the cold climate areas there are sometimes years when camellia flowers are pollinated and seeds are set quite freely out in the garden. Otherwise the warmth of an unheated glasshouse makes all the difference, with man having to take control and carry out the pollination artificially.

Artificial pollination

The serious, scientific camellia breeder will select both seed and pollen parents, each of which has some particular features which he/she wishes to combine in the offspring. It may be the habit, leaf shape or colour, flower colour or form, or perfume. A basic knowledge of genetics is helpful, together with information about the chromosome counts of different camellia species and therefore their compatibility. It is beyond the scope of this book to go into this in any detail, but a start can be made from the following information.

New cultivars can be produced by using, for example, two existing cultivars or varieties of *C. japonica*, in which case the seedlings will be more cultivars of *C. japonica,* or parents can be chosen from the background of two different species in which case the seedlings will be hybrids. There is more scope to produce something new when working with the latter, and with the further stage of back crossing the progeny. For example, a *C. japonica* variety was crossed with *C. saluenensis* to produce an *williamsii* hybrid, eg 'Blue Danube'. This was back crossed with a *C. japonica* variety, eg 'Raspberry Delight', to produce a new hybrid: 'Waltz Time'.

Having selected the parent plants, whether planted outdoors in warm climates, or in pots under glass in cooler regions, possible flowers are chosen just as they begin to open. The best stage is before the stamens or stigma are clearly visible. Outdoors it is better to choose the flowers which are to be seed parents from under the shelter of other branches. The traditional method is to cut away all the petals of the chosen seed parent flower, sufficient to be able to see the stigma and stamens clearly and to remove all the stamens so that no pollen will be produced. It should then be enclosed in a paper bag and tied securely to the branch, to prevent the bees taking any old pollen onto the stigma. (Plastic bags are not recommended, especially in warm climates as the humid atmosphere encourages condensation.) The pollen parent does not need any treatment as it is only necessary to gather its pollen. This can best be done by cutting the flower before the pollen ripens and taking it into a bee-proof room to ripen it. Ripe pollen is powdery and can be collected with a soft paintbrush. It can either be transferred directly onto the stigma of the chosen seed parent, or, if it is to be used on a later flowering variety, it can be stored in the fridge in a small, jar or one of those little black film containers until the seed parent flower is ready. Pollen can even be posted to fellow camellia breeders across the world.

The bag should be kept in place around the now, hopefully, fertilised flower for at least a week after pollination to make sure no unwanted pollen from another source reaches the stigma. A lock label or similar will be needed to attach the name of the pollen parent on the branch close to the fertilized flower and the union recorded for future reference. It is surprising how easy it is to forget such things, especially as the 'hybridising bug' can become very addictive and many plants about the garden will probably be decorated with paper bags. Correctly the seed parent is always written first and the pollen parent second, so a cross using the pollen of C. japonica 'Bob Hope' on the stigma of C. x williamsii 'Donation' is recorded thus: C. x williamsii 'Donation' xC. japonica 'Bob Hope'.

Seed development and germination

Once fertilised, the seeds develop inside the fruit. This development should be closely monitored as they start splitting, so one can collect the seeds before they drop and the mice get them. Squirrels and other mammals, even some birds such as parrots in Australian gardens, will readily take the seeds. (Their favourites seem to be the fruit of C. yunnanensis.)

In warm climates the hopefully fertile seeds should be dipped in fungicide and sown straight away, outdoors to a depth of no more than 1cm in the seed compost, in pots or trays kept in a rodent proof box in a shady area. The seed compost should be sterile: peat/perlite as a 50 : 50 mix is good, or straight peat if drainage is certain to be good. The seeds will germinate naturally when conditions are right, usually in the spring.

In cooler areas such as in the UK the seeds are best dipped in fungicide and kept cool but frostproof in sterile moist peat or sphagnum during the winter, in a rodent proof, well ventilated box. In early spring they can be placed in a propagator, or in the airing cupboard provided it is not too hot, to germinate. In these somewhat forced conditions germination will start quickly and small roots may appear within three or four weeks. Tap roots may, if desired, be trimmed back to about 5cm. And then the seedlings are potted up in the same way as any small plant, but these will not yet have shoots and the cotyledons should be placed on the surface of the compost or only just under it. No fertilizer is needed at this stage, but the seedlings should be kept in a warm, light but shaded place. The two fleshy cotyledons will continue to supply each seedling with nourishment until leaves develop to take over, which will be in another two or three weeks. Feeding with a very dilute liquid fertilizer can start three or four weeks after this and, as it will now be summer, the plants gradually hardened off. They will need nursery protection in winter for another couple of years, and to be potted up into larger pots as they grow, in the normal way. After four years they should flower and their worth can be assessed after another two or three years. Breeders need to be a patient race.

5

Exibiting Camellias

There is no doubt that exhibiting camellias at shows gives a great deal of pleasure, both to the exhibitor and to the people who go to wonder and enjoy the spectacle. Prizes are often small, but the camaraderie amongst exhibitors, and the friendships made as a result of the friendly rivalry which usually exists at such events, is worth the effort. In Britain the regular March and April shows at the RHS Halls at Vincent Square in London always have competitive classes for camellias as well as for other shrubs and for daffodils.

In Australia and New Zealand there are camellia shows organised by local branches of the Australian and New Zealand Camellia Societies, and a National Show once a year in a location which changes from year to year.

In the USA, with dozens of camellia societies in the states where camellias are grown (California has ten such societies), the shows are the main focus of the year, with with some exhibitors travelling from show to show, making it a real way of life for the few months of the flowering season. In the more southerly areas, where petal blight is a major problem the practice of gibbing enables blooms to be ready to show much earlier than their natural flowering season, thus avoiding the problem of damaged blooms which are such a problem when temperatures rise in the spring. South Georgia and South Carolina have shows exhibiting varieties of *C. japonica* grown outdoors as early as October, and not all the blooms are gibbed!

Dedicated exhibitors grow their plants specifically to produce 'show' blooms. Plants are heavily pruned to ensure well spread flowers. Buds are removed, leaving just one at each site.

There are usually classes for novices and plenty of help is given to first-time exhibitors when they arrive at their first show, both by stewards and by more experienced competitors.

WHAT THE JUDGES LOOK FOR

Different criteria apply in each region but the following are widely accepted.

Show camellias ready for transport, using wood wool as a packing material

Well-spaced show camellias arriving in their cardboard box

The New Zealand Camellia Society holds superb camellia shows

1 Is the bloom 'according to schedule'? It should be of the correct flower form 'on the day', and may not necessarily conform to the description of the flower in the catalogue of the nursery it was supplied by, or even in the *International Register*. *C. japonica* 'Grand Slam' may, for example, have both semi-double and anemone form flowers on the same bush at the same time but an anemone form bloom entered in a semi-double class may be marked 'NAS' (Not According to Schedule) and eliminated by the judges. It is worth checking before staging blooms. In classes where size is defined the blooms should be measured to ensure that they fall into the right category. The main difficulty arises with the definitions of 'small' and 'miniature', and 'large' and 'very large'. For classes for named varieties it is, of course, important to check that your entry is

correctly named.

2   Blooms should be fresh.

3   Blooms should be undamaged, with no sign of bruising.

4   Blooms should be fully open, but not about to drop. There is nothing worse than to see your prized specimen sitting on the table beside its container as the judges approach.

5   The care taken to display the blooms to their best advantage is important. There is a certain undefinable 'something' about this, which can only be described as flair. Some people have it naturally, others acquire it.

SOME TIPS

When selecting blooms for show, cut them in the cool of the evening, or early morning. Look in the middle, or on the lower branches for blooms. They are usually less exposed to damage and of a good colour. There are many ways of caring for camellia flowers between cutting and benching at the show. Most people keep them in individual pots, in water, sometimes with a little sugar, or dissolved aspirin, or a florist's proprietary preservative, overnight, in a cool dark room. For travelling, many use cool boxes; especially those in warm climates or those travelling far. Others use large cardboard boxes acquired from the local florist. Blooms may then be transported either well-spaced and upright with their stems in orchid tubes (small glass tubes like laboratory test tubes), which can be held in a rigid wooden rack with holes, or well spaced and laid flattish on a bed of shredded newspaper, tissue paper, wood shavings or other material to stop them sliding about as they travel. Cut stems may be enclosed in moist cotton wool or moss, held in place with a strip of polythene and an elastic band. Take secateurs, florist's foam, if permitted (to hold the blooms upright in the containers), tweezers and fine-pointed nail scissors (to remove any discoloured or damaged flower parts such as the odd stamen or petaloid stamen), a fine paint brush, or camera lens puffer brush (to chase away specks of dust or pollen which have landed on petals); pen, paper, scissors and white card in case you need to write cultivar labels to identify your blooms in classes where they are not already named.

Keep the boxes as cool as possible while in transit.

Arrive early. Check in and collect any paperwork. Have a look round the hall to see where your blooms are to be shown. Benching tables are usually provided for exhibitors to use to sort and arrange their blooms in the containers, which are usually provided. These get congested as the time to clear the hall for judging approaches. Stage/bench your blooms with care, avoiding dropping water on the benches or knocking other peoples' exhibits.

Clear up and remove all debris from the benching tables.

Disappear and await the judges' decisions! The above are just suggestions. Experienced exhibitors will already have their own tricks of the trade, and could no doubt add much more.

Judging criteria also vary, with countries where showing is on a large scale having trainee judging schemes and a more structured approach compared to others. The main thing is to show for pleasure.

6

Problems, Pests
And Diseases

Camellias are incredibly tolerant and trouble-free shrubs, but symptoms do appear every now and again and cause puzzlement or concern. Some are due to pests or diseases which may spread and cause more trouble, while others are caused by cultural conditions which are not transmitted to other plants and include some which may be due to weather conditions which are beyond the control of any gardener.

Physiological disorders and fungal problems are less likely to occur with plants that are healthy and kept growing well. Camellias which are starved, waterlogged, overcrowded, or otherwise neglected or over-treated are far more vulnerable than plants which do not experience excesses or extremes. Prevention is always better than cure.

PHYSIOLOGICAL DISORDERS

Leaves
Symptoms: Yellowing of leaves – chlorosis.

Old age: All camellias, despite their term 'evergreen', develop yellow leaves, especially towards the centre of older plants. They turn yellow from the central vein outwards before developing brown patches and dropping off the plant. Provided these symptoms are not excessive they can be ignored and accepted as a perfectly natural process.

Nitrogen deficiency: Nitrogen deficiency causes similar symptoms, but these are exhibited over the whole plant.

Iron deficiency causes yellowing between the veins.

Deficiencies such as nitrogen and iron may be due to lack of fertilizer in the soil or due to either a shortage or an excess of water which prevents the roots taking the fertilizers into the plant. (More detailed information about these and other mineral deficiencies is found under 'The vital elements'.)

Chlorosis in patches or irregular blotches is likely to be due to virus.

Curling, twisted roots are often the result on camellias which have been pot bound

One solution is to cut the woody roots off to encourage a more fibrous root system

A pale plant which fails to thrive indicates trouble at the roots

Weather damage

Symptoms: Leaves develop discoloured patches on the upper surface, between the veins, which may be brown or bleached, and give the leaf a semi-blistered appearance due to the destruction of cells in the leaf. Identification can be confirmed by looking at the leaves below. They may be a healthy glossy green where they are partially protected by the shadow of the scorched leaves above and damaged where they are exposed.

Sun scorch is most damaging on some varieties of *C. japonica*. It happens when plants are either exposed to bright sun and hot conditions, or in winter if there is a combination of sun, wind and frost. Some varieties are more prone than others.

Remedy: If a variety is suffering in the garden at present and giving no pleasure it should either be moved to a more shaded site or dug out, disposed of, and replaced with a sun-resistant variety recommended by your nursery supplier.

Soil salts damage

Symptoms: Browning of the leaves, starting near the tips of the outer margins and working its way inwards. This is seen at any time of the year on plants which have an imbalance of fertilizer or excess of other salts in the soil or compost and particularly if there is insufficient water to dilute them. It is more of a problem in winter or early spring, before growth starts, on plants in containers which have a build up of excess

Sun scorch (Australia)

fertilizers which, because of winter inactivity, the plants cannot absorb. It causes root damage which is not apparent until the subsequent damage to the leaves occurs. It is often worst on plants which have been fed late in the growing season with an excess of fertilizer with a high concentration of potash and just too little nitrogen.

Remedy: Raise the pots to allow maximum drainage and flush through with clear water to remove the excess minerals. In subsequent years feed with a more balanced fertilizer, in moderation, and not too late in the growing season.

Corky scab or oedema

Symptoms: Small raised bumps on the under side of older leaves, which appear to have a tough-looking cover. Another name for this condition is 'scurf', which describes the appearance well. The cause is not fully understood but is probably due to sudden changes in climate or watering, for example when too much water is suddenly supplied on a dull day following a period of hot sunny weather and relative dryness. It appears as if cells, particularly on the under side of leaves, have been swollen with too much water which they are

unable to use for their own food manufacture (photosynthesis) or to get rid of by transpiration. Groups of cells appear to form a covering callus. It is seen more on camellias with leathery leaves such as some *C. reticulata* varieties and their hybrids.

The disease is unsightly but not infectious, and gradually becomes less obvious as the plant grows and younger leaves obscure the damage.

Remedy: There is no remedy except to try to avoid the conditions described above.

Excessive leaf drop

This is almost always due to trouble at the roots, usually too much or too little water, overfeeding or other mineral imbalance and follows other signs such as changes in leaf colour. It can occur on camellias which have been brought suddenly into hot dry conditions, in which case it will happen in a matter of days, or those which have had frozen roots in which case it may not become apparent until the roots are required for action in spring, maybe months later.

Flower bud drop

This probably causes more worry and frustration to new camellia enthusiasts than any other camellia problem. It is natural for some camellias to lose a few flower buds, especially those which form an abundance, in order that the plant can do justice to the remainder. However, there is nothing more disheartening than watching flower buds form, begin to swell and then drop off, forming a carpet under the plant which promised so much for the following spring. Damage on this scale is likely to occur when temperatures drop to below -12°C for more than a few days. It may also happen in less severe winter conditions, more often because of lack of water at the crucial time when flower buds are forming and becoming established in late summer or autumn.

If there is a break in the supply of water to the cells forming and arranging themselves into a flower stalk they will not function properly; there will be malformation and therefore a point of weakness. This will be found out either at the first sign of stress, when the first real frost of winter occurs, or as the buds start to swell before flowering. Container-grown camellias are more vulnerable than those in the ground, and some varieties are more prone than others.

Remedy: Pay particular attention to watering in late summer and autumn while flower buds are forming, and, if conditions are particularly hot and dry, spray cool water over soil and surroundings – and if not too sunny, over foliage also. Avoid varieties which are known to be prone to bud drop, especially in cold climate areas.

Flower bud balling

This is a situation where the flower buds appear ready to burst forth into bloom, but fail to open and eventually rot. It happens in spring weather which is particularly warm, dry and desiccating, or where frost has damaged outer petals as they begin to emerge from the protection of the bud scales. The damaged tissues, surround and

It is disheartening to find a carpet of flower buds on the ground after the first frost

prevent the expansion of the inner flower.

Remedy: None, except the prompt removal of affected buds to prevent the fungal infections, which attack the dead tissues, spreading to adjacent, healthy buds.

FUNGAL DISEASES

These are relatively few, particularly on plants in cooler climates where fungal spores do not germinate rapidly. They cause more problems in warmer areas of high humidity or in a glass house or other protected area. Having well spaced plants with good air circulation around them helps to prevent fungal problems. Specific fungicides are not mentioned, as regulations and availability vary so much in each country. Instructions should always be read and followed carefully and all safety measures taken.

Honey fungus (*Armillarea mellea*)

This fungus is universal and often endemic in gardens created on land previously used as woodland as it is one of the most efficient means of rotting dead or dying trees in the natural order of things. The problem is that it does not always

Remaining flower buds may have damaged bud scales, but the flower inside may be undamaged

stop there because it will sometimes invade the root systems of some types of apparently healthy trees and shrubs, including camellias.

Symptoms: Affected camellias will stop thriving and start to look generally sick over a period of several months, or even longer, with a drooping and generally pale and lethargic look about them. Sometimes only one side of a bush is affected to start with.

The fungus spreads from rotting old tree stumps or roots under the ground, or from other infected living trees or shrubs, by means of root-like brown threads (rhizomorphs) which turn black with age, and look like old fashioned boot laces. These have a slight elasticity when stretched, unlike roots which do not stretch in the same way, and can be found about 13cm below the surface of the ground. Only the paler young tips which form from the multi-branched ends of the rhizomorphs are actively feeding. They cause damage as they feed by giving out digestive juices which first kill the living part of woody roots before moving on to the rest. These active tips make their way up the root system, gradually weakening it as they do so, until, usually a year or more later, the camellia may be killed completely, although many live in a state of unhealthy suspended animation for years.

The fungus reproduces sexually by giving out spores from groups of yellow mushroom-like toadstools which can be seen at the foot of tree stumps or other dead wood, or growing apparently from the ground – in reality from rhizomorphs below. Mid-autumn is the time to look for them. They can sometimes be smelt before being seen as they give off a sweet, honey-like smell.

Remedy: Because of the importance of Armillarea to the forestry industry there have been strenuous efforts to try to find a remedy, so far without success. The only means of control seems to be to remove all tree and shrub stumps as they are felled and to collect and burn them and all other dead wood before they start rotting. Various chemicals have been used but these are not yet of proven worth on a general scale. It is generally accepted that vigorously growing camellias are less likely to be affected.

Twig blight, canker, die-back (Glomerella cingulata)

This fungus, although not at all common in cool climate areas, can be a very significant problem in glasshouses everywhere, and can be a major problem outdoors in warm climates with high humidity as in the southern States of the USA and in parts of Australia. It does not usually occur outdoors in Britain and other cool climate areas nor in hot dry climates. It is somewhat selective, with many C. *saluenensis* hybrids (*williamsii*), and some varieties of C. *japonica*, C. *reticulata*, C. *sasanqua* and their hybrids suffering more than others.

Symptoms: The first signs are usually on the current year's young growth, which wilts without any apparent reason. On very young growth, leaves fall off quite quickly, while the leaves on slightly older shoots wilt, then turn brown before falling off. The fungus attacks the cells at the base of shoots, damaging the water supply, which causes the wilting. If it is allowed to develop, the next stage is the attack on the woody cells up and down the stem from the original site, destroying as it goes, causing a sunken area of infected wood – the canker. Healthy wood around this area remains, but the canker is the breeding ground for the next generation for the future spread of the disease.

Remedy: As the fungus is known to enter the plant through wounds, including leaf scars, it is wise to use a suitable fungicide whenever cuts are made, during propagation or pruning, for example. Good ventilation and spacing both around and within the plants will help to avoid infection, but in areas where *Glomerella* is a major problem it might be necessary to avoid growing varieties of known susceptibility, combined with an efficient fungicide programme for the rest.

A less virulent fungus, *Phenopsis spp.* causes cankers in hot, dry climates such as California. Varietites of *C. reticulata* and *C. sansanqua* appeal to be more susceptible than varieties of *C. japonica*, especially when under stress.

Leaf spot

This may be caused by two different fungi: *Pestalotiopsis guepini* or *Monochaetia camelliae*. Both are more likely on leaves which have been physically damaged in some way, and on plants which are 'soft' grown on a high nutrient diet under glass, for example. These fungal infections often follow cell damage from sunscorch, or from cutting leaves in half at propagation.

Symptoms: *Pestalotiopsis* shows as silvery grey spots on the upper surface of leaves, with a lighter brown colour underneath. Small black dots on these areas contain the spores for reproduction. *Monochaetia* is very similar, but appears in circles which spread outwards as the infection spreads.

Remedy: Remove all infected material if possible and burn. Use a fungicide drench to kill remaining infection. When physical injury has occurred, use a fungicide spray as a routine, in anticipation of a possible infection, especially under glasshouse conditions.

Camellia leaf gall (Exobasidium species)

Much more dramatic in appearance than in significance, these hideous galls may appear in summer or early autumn.

Symptoms: Tryffid-like, often quite large (10cm or more), the galls are white or greyish and appear amongst the foliage of camellias in most countries. There is seldom more than one in any garden, probably as they are so obvious that they are removed before they ripen and release their spores, which are distributed by the wind.

Remedy: Remove and burn.

Sooty mould

Probably the most common, and certainly the

Die-back (*Glomerella cingulata*) can be a problem where humidity is high

Camellia leaf galls look like something from a science-fiction story, but do little damge

most unsightly fungal disease on camellias and other evergreens. It is not in itself harmful except when infection is on a large scale, in which case it prevents light for food manufacture from reaching the leaf tissues. It is secondary to attack by insects such as scale insects, aphids, and any other sap sucking insects, which produce the sticky, sweet excreta known as honeydew upon which the mould fungus thrives.

Symptoms: Patches of grey-black appear on the upper surface of leaves. This usually happens between spring and late autumn or when it is warm enough for insects to be active and feeding.

Remedy: Control of the insect pest comes first, after that, the removal of the mould. fungus. Fungicide sprays may be used, but although they may kill the mould, they are unlikely to remove it promptly as it is firmly attached to the sticky honeydew. The usual method is to do it by hand, using a sponge or soft cloth and clean water. Detergents should be used with care as the waxy covering to the leaves may be dissolved by them. If the problem is too large then patience and hosing over frequently with clean water will eventually do the trick.

Camellia root rot (Phytopthora cinnamomi)

Root rot used to be more of a problem in the past, but with the increase in use of soilless composts, which tend to have better drainage, and greater attention to hygiene in nurseries, it has decreased in significance. It can, however, occur, especially in young plants, where soil conditions are compacted and become waterlogged. It may also be a problem if dirty water is used, especially if it has been recycled untreated from run-off from other plants in a water conservation scheme.

Symptoms: These tend to appear in early spring and can often be confused with frost damage to roots. Yellowing of young leaves and dying back from the tips of branches is the first sign. If there are no healthy white roots, the plant has not been subjected to freezing conditions and the soil is soggy and compacted, then the root rot fungus can probably be blamed.

Remedy: Once a container-grown camellia has been identified as suffering from root rot, most of the soil should be removed, the roots then dipped into a bucket of fungicide, and then the plant

Sooty mould fungus is common everywhere and unsightly, but not life threatening

should be repotted in fresh, sterile compost of more open consistency. Larger, open ground plants may need to have soil removed from around their root area and beyond, to allow for future expansion, trimming of damaged roots with a sharp knife, then a fungicide drench used to fill the resultant trench, and more open, clean, compost used to fill it once it has drained completely. Alternatively plants may be lifted, have their roots trimmed and treated, and then be potted up in containers in good compost.

Flower or petal blight (Ciborinia camelliae)

Flower blight affects camellia blooms in parts of the world where high temperatures and humidity occur. It has been recognised in China and Japan and in California and the southern States of the USA since 1938. In 1993 it appeared in New Zealand for the first time, in the Wellington area. Damage is solely to flowers but it does not spread from flower to flower. It is also easily confused with Botrytis, which is common on flowers in hot humid conditions everywhere.

Symptoms: Flower blight, unlike other fungi,

attacks blooms as they open, with petals first showing a rusty brown colour and a 'veininess' in appearance. The brown colour spreads rapidly from the centre outwards, and the whole flower may be brown in three days with the tips of the petals usually the last part to go brown. The flower may be dead in five days. What distinguishes this disease from Botrytis is the fact that it does not produce spores on the flower, but if an infected flower is examined, a ring of fine threads (hyphae) like a cotton wool collar, may be seen around the base of the petals where they were attached to the flower stalk. Damage from frost and wind can, of course, cause browning, but this usually starts from the outer part of the petals and is initially paler brown.

If flower blight is not quickly detected and dealt with the flower falls to the ground and the ring of fungal tissue at the base of the petals hardens to form a hard black, potential fruiting body (sclerotium) in about two weeks. This gets covered by leaves and other debris and may lie dormant for several years, but may germinate early in the following spring. When it does so it grows out to form small (1cm) tan-coloured mushroom like bodies (apothecia). These, when ripe, forcefully eject millions of spores into the air. They can be carried in the air for up to 2km, but are more likely to travel about 200 metres. This happens in mid to late spring, just as the majority of camellia varieties are in full bloom. Once spores land on an opening flower they grow out into threads, and the cycle repeats itself.

Remedy: There is no recommended spray at the time of writing. Prevention is very important if flower blight is not already present. The plant health authorities of Britain, Australia and other countries free of the disease will not accept camellias from areas known to be infected without rigorous assurances from the compulsory inspection in the exporting country, and certain basic ground rules must be followed in order to qualify for a Plant Health Certificate. These include: no flowers, flower buds, or soil, on plants or scions and fumigation is insisted upon in Australia.

If flower blight is suspected in an as yet uninfected area or country it should immediately be reported to the Ministry of Agriculture. Control measures used in already infected areas include picking up and burning all infected blooms, with polythene mulch used to see and collect them more easily. It also helps to prevent the black sclerotia settling into the soil and becoming hidden. Good weed control also helps. It will do no harm and may even help to drench the opening flowers with a general fungicide from early spring, repeating this every 14 days during the flowering season. It is hoped that a specific fungicide may be recommended in time.

Flower spot (Botrytis cinerea)

Botrytis is a common fungal disease in cool humid conditions and infests older or dead and dying flowers. It can be distinguished from flower blight by the paler brown of the damaged flowers,

and the presence of spores which are relatively easily detectable amongst the older damaged petals, and around the base of the petals.

Remedy: Improve ventilation. Regular use of a fungicide may be necessary if conditions remain cold and humid.

VIRUS DISEASES

Camellia viruses have come close to causing international friction because they can actually cause, by deliberate inoculation, the creation of new forms of existing varieties by adding spots and blotches which in the eyes of some, enhance the appearance of the blooms. *C.x williamsii* 'Anticipation variegated' is an example. It, and many others win prizes on the show benches in some countries because of their eye-catching colours, but they are frowned upon in others.

The word 'virus' means 'poison' in Latin, so any virus can be regarded as an invasive intrusion upon the normal healthy life of whatever organism it occupies. Camellia viruses are no different, but, as with the common cold virus, they are not unduly debilitating or even noticeable in all carriers. They can keep a camellia in a below par state, so that it lacks vigour; this is particularly so with some of the old plants of varieties of *C. japonica* in Europe, and of many of the Yunnan *reticulata*s imported in the past. They can also inhibit rooting during propagation.

PESTS

Specific chemicals are not recommended as their availability changes constantly in all countries. When choosing and using chemical insecticides the presence of other beneficial insects such as bees, as well as the natural predators of the pests, should be borne in mind, not forgetting the birds. More 'safe' insecticides are now on the market, with many based on the old, tried and tested natural product: Pyrethrin. All instructions should be read carefully and due care taken when handling any chemicals, and spraying done early in the morning or in the evening in still air.

Vine Weevil (Otiorhynchus sulcatus)

This is a particularly troublesome pest in young container grown plants, including camellias, especially under glass, and especially where pot-grown cyclamen, primula and other herbaceous plants are also kept. Adults are seen in warm conditions such as this in early autumn. Outdoors, they do not emerge until late spring/early summer in Britain.

The adults are all female, about 9mm in length, black with fine yellow speckles on the rough textured wing cases. They rest in the daytime under the rims of pots, under leaves, or in any other shelter. At night, particularly (so the research entomologists tell us), between the hours of 11pm and 1am, they are active and can run with great speed. They feed on the leaves of camellias and other plants, making characteristic rounded notches which are different from those left by other leaf-eating beetles. These are unsightly but not particularly damaging.

Each adult can lay about 1,500 eggs in batches in leaf litter on the soil near suitable host plants, or in odd cracks and crannies nearby. This is done outdoors in late summer, with resultant grubs overwintering in the soil, burrowing down amongst the roots of host plants. They feed voraciously on the roots and grow actively when the weather warms up in spring. They are legless, with a curved white body, and a brown head. Under glass, eggs are mostly laid from spring through summer, with resultant grubs actively feeding on roots throughout the summer before emerging as adults in autumn, or in the following spring. It takes between 12 and 18 months to complete the life cycle.

Healthy, tender, white root systems of young camellias are particularly susceptible, including those just produced in the propagating bench. The first signs of trouble are often collapsed plants, which when examined are seen to have very little, if any, root system left. Sometimes the bark around the stem, just below ground level, is chewed round (or ringed), breaking off the water supply from the roots to the shoots.

Control: Many gardeners claim success by going out at night, with a lamp, as soon as notched leaves appear, and catching and killing the adults by hand. Insecticide sprays seldom work because the protective coating of the weevils is so effective.

The larvae are also targeted. In the garden larvae may be kept under control by other natural predators such as birds. It is wise to examine the compost of newly acquired plants in pots; larvae tend to be found right in the middle and should be removed and destroyed. As an added precaution the soil and roots may be immersed in a bucket of water for a few hours. This apparently drowns the larvae.

The main artificial method is the use of sponges impregnated with live parasitic nematodes. (They are available by mail order.) These are squeezed out in the recommended amount of clean water, which is then used to drench the infected pots or soil.

The nematodes enter the body of each vine weevil larva by any orifice. They carry their own food source with them (bacteria), so they feed and multiply within the larvae, killing each within two days. They are only active between 10°C and 30°C.

Mature camellias are not too troubled by pests, most of which are kept down to acceptable levels by natural predators, or are so transient in activity that it is simpler to tolerate them than to

Yellow spots and blotches caused by Leaf Mottle Virus

Birds can tear petals in their search for the nectar at their base

attack them. Occasionally it is necessary to use positive control measures.

The following are pests which can build up to unacceptable levels:

Sap-sucking armoured scale insects

There may be five or six types which affect camellias around the world. In the UK they are a nuisance, not so much because of serious direct harm, but because of their excreta (honeydew) upon which the unsightly sooty mould fungus grows. They can be found on the underside of leaves. There is often no sign of them on the upper surface, although pin prick damage may be seen if their sucking has reached the tissues in this area.

In warm climates, the damage may be more severe, with two types, the Tea Scale and the Florida red scale, being particularly damaging. Both leaf surfaces are damaged.

Scale insects are protected at maturity by a covering which is usually shell-like. The females live under this and are relatively immobile. In winter they congregate along the veins near the leaf stalk, or even down this onto the stem. In summer they move up to the under-side of the lamina of the leaf and start feeding by sucking the sap, and do not move thereafter, laying their eggs under the armour, and eventually dying.

Control: Insecticide sprays should be directed to the under side of leaves, and may need to be repeated several times as the protective armour covering the soft body of the insects is very effective. Feeding starts in spring, which is a good time for the first spray. Populations build up in early autumn and need to be dealt with before the insects stop feeding and become dormant under their particularly protective winter overcoats.

Natural predators such as ladybird beetles, and small birds like goldfinches and tits are excellent controllers so a careful decision should be made before spraying.

Aphids

These often attack young growth, especially under glass and can rapidly build up to epidemic proportions. If not promptly controlled, the leaves will always be distorted and unsightly.

Sooty mould also settles on the honeydew produced by these sap sucking insects.

Control: A strong jet of water will dislodge most, but a few remaining ones may need to be removed by hand. An insecticide spray may be needed for severe infestation.

Mites

These may thrive in warm environments. Red mites appear as a fine red dust on the under side of leaves, often accompanied by a web akin to that of their spider relatives. They suck sap and may be both debilitating and, as with other sap sucking creatures, produce honeydew.

Control: Under glass, if beneficial insects are not present, use an insecticide smoke or spray. Occasionally the cause of flower bud scale browning or failure of buds to open, especially if under glass or in warm climates, may be traced to bud mite. These mites are difficult to detect.

Control: If suspected, a regular preventative insecticide spraying programme is recommended during autumn as the buds swell.

Leaf-eating beetles

Rhabdopterus sp. and the New Zealand grass grub *Costelytra zealandica* attack young camellia leaves from spring through summer in warm climates, leaving holes and notches which have a shape characteristic of each genus.

Control: This will only be necessary in severe infestations. They feed at night, so an insecticide spray, applied then or very late in the evening to both the leaves and the leaf litter under the plants can be effective.

Thrips

These sap sucking insects are rarely a problem, but sometimes attack camellia leaves causing speckling and, because they leave the cell contents empty, the leaves develop a silvered appearance. Defoliation can occur in a severe attack. *C. sasanqua* varieties appear to be favoured, and the problem is greater in warm climates.

Control: Natural predators are few so spraying with insecticide is necessary.

Other minor pests

These are unlikely to become too troublesome and should largely be tolerated. They are best controlled by removal by hand, or by cutting out localised invasion. Occasionally an insecticide may be needed.

Looper caterpillars feed on young growth, but may be controlled by insecticide spraying as are caterpillars which can destroy flower buds.

Leaf roller caterpillars may be found inside rolls of immature camellia leaves. They are best controlled by squashing.

Leaf miners occasionally burrow under camellia leaves surfaces. Control by removal of individual leaves, or if the attack is severe, use a systemic insecticide – not in the flowering season.

Larger pests

Deer have a fondness for camellia leaves, and rabbits eat both the leaves and chew the stems. The only effective remedy is to erect a fence, but plastic tree guards are excellent for protecting individual bushes or trees.

Nectar seeking birds may damage flowers with beaks and claws as they seek the nectar at the base of camellia petals. In the UK it is a transient problem, with the mid-winter flowering varieties like *C .x williamsii*, 'Bow Bells' very attractive to blue tits in the first few weeks of its long flowering season.

Mice and other rodents may seek out the biggest, fattest buds on the lower branches of camellias, especially under glass.

PROBLEMS, PESTS AND DISEASES UNDER GLASS

Pests and diseases enjoy the protected environment of a glasshouse and a close watch needs to be kept for them. There are also some physiological problems which are not harmful in the same way but can cause blemishes. All are dealt with in full earlier, but those that are particularly damaging in protected environments are listed here.

Physiological problems

Most of these are due to climatic conditions which occur outdoors in some of the warmer climates where similar conditions may occur under cold glasshouse conditions in cooler climate areas.

Corky scab, or oedema, can best be prevented by avoiding irregular watering and sudden rises or drops in temperature or humidity under glass. Sun scorch is common in early summer if shading is not put over early enough.

Salt injury or conductivity problems are more common in container-grown plants under glass. Excess fertilizer in their compost should be flushed out with clean water.

Mice and other rodent damage is common in early spring, when fat flower buds disappear from the camellias and are subsequently found in small caches in odd corners in the glasshouse.

Fungal diseases

Flower blight (*Sclerotinia camelliae*) in countries where it is endemic.

Die-back (*Glomerella cingulata*) is largely prevented by good management to encourage good air circulation plus avoiding late ripening of young growth by ceasing feeding by late summer.

Leaf spot (*Pestalotiopsis guepini*) which occurs after some physical damage, such as when leaves are cut across during propagation.

Botrytis cinerea is responsible for brown discolouration of flowers and can be avoided by allowing good ventilation. It can be confused with flower blight.

Root rot (*Phytopthora cinnamomi*) which causes destruction of roots in wet, compacted compost. The use of clean or new pots, sterilised compost, well aerated and uncompacted at potting, plus clean water reduces the risk.

Insect pests

Aphids are often a problem on young growth under glass, with two major periods of infestation. One as shoots burst into growth in spring, and the second when the brown aphids attack young leaves in late summer.

Woolly aphids, with their tendency to cluster on stems and axils of leaves of camellias under glass, covered by their protective, waxy coating, are difficult to control once established.

Scale insects which come in three or four different forms according to the country. These sucking insects build up quickly in warm conditions and a close watch must be kept out for them, especially in autumn in unheated houses as they are very difficult to eradicate once cold conditions start and they build their protective coating around them. As with insect pests outdoors, prompt action using an insecticide is important once the first sign of 'honeydew' or the sooty mould which follows it are seen. Under glass the use of smokes is possible and very effective.

Vine weevil damage is often severe if these insects are present, but more easily controlled under glass as adult damage is quickly seen before they lay their eggs in summer. Larvae are more easily controlled by biological means in the warm temperatures under glass, but are themselves killed if the temperature rises above 32°C.

6

Camellia Varieties

This is just a small selection of the varieties available at the time of writing. They are divided into groups according to their species origins, dealing first with just over 100 cultivars of *C. japonica*, followed by 40 *williamsii* varieties, 18 large-flowered *reticulata* hybrids, 24 *sasanqua*s and 27 assorted hybrids with parentage from a variety of species. Conditions throughout the world differ greatly but some idea of the flowering season size, colour and flower type are given as well as the general growth habit and the type of aspect where each should be happy. Hardiness ratings are indicated.

FLOWERING SEASONS
Very early = autumn–early winter
Early = winter–early spring
Mid-season = mid-spring
Late = late spring

SUGGESTED SITE ASPECTS
Full sun acceptable – ○
Semi shade preferred – ◑

Full shade acceptable – ●

Depending on the micro-climate of the site many varieties will succeed in aspects other than those indicated. Allowances need to be made in extremes of climate.

HARDINESS RATINGS
These give some indication of the temperatures which each variety is likely to withstand without being severely affected or killed. These are for reasonably sheltered sites where low temperatures are not experienced for long periods.

Hardy *** Hardy down to -15°C to -20°C
Frost hardy ** Hardy down to -10°C
Tender * Damage expected below -2°C

FLOWER SIZES
Miniature – 6cm or less
Small – 6 to 7.5cm
Medium – 7.5–10cm
Large – 10–13cm
Very large – over 13cm

FLOWER TYPES (INTERNATIONAL CAMELLIA REGISTER)

Single one row of not over eight petals which can be regular, irregular or loosely arranged about a central conspicuous stamen cluster, but without petaloids. The Japanese, who particularly favour the beauty and simplicity of the singles, have further sub-divided them into six classes (See *International Camellia Register*)

Semi double In excess of eight petals in two or more rows with a conspicuous stamen centre, with no petaloids. The petals may be regular, irregular or loose. In Japan the semi-doubles are divided into three types

Anemone form One or more rows of large petals with a convex mass of petaloid stamens in the centre. There are two types: the typical form being small and having one row of outer petals and a very compact centre. The second type is larger, having two or three rows of outer petals and a more open central mass, sometimes with as many small petals as petaloids

peony form There are two types: the first being the loose peony which has loosely arranged petals which are smaller towards the centre where stamens and petaloids intermingle with them. The second type, the 'full peony' has a mass of irregular twisted petals and petaloids with no obvious stamens

Rose form double Many rows of imbricated petals with some stamens visible in the centre of the flower when fully mature

Formal double Many rows of regular overlapping petals with no stamens

Some varieties exhibit two or more flower forms on the same bush at the same time and others may be peony form in hot climates but rose form or formal double in cooler areas.

FLOWER COLOUR

The colour given of a particular variety is normally thee colour registered by the introducer, but the author has used her own experience to make comments in some cases. It may vary according to soil, climate, season and stage of maturity of the bloom.

VARIETIES OF *CAMELLIA JAPONICA*

'Adelina Patti'. Brought to England from Japan in 1888 and still winning prizes. The single flowers pink edged white with carmine venation and shading towards the base of the rounded petals. The leaves are a deep, glossy green on an upright bush. ◖ **

'Adolphe Audusson'. First obtained in about 1877 by the Henri Guichard nursery in Nantes, France, from M. Adolphe Audusson of Angers, it was originally listed in the *Guichard* catalogue in 1910. The flowers are a bright red, semi-double of medium to large size, mid-season. The bush grows big, bold and densely bushy, with handsome, dark green leaves. A reliable old favourite. ◖● ***

'Akashigata' ('Lady Clare'). Introduced from Japan in 1859 and renamed by the Caldonian Nursery in Guernsey, Channel Islands. The flowers open in mid-season and are deep reddish pink on a vigorous bush, with large, elliptical leaves. ○◖● ***

'Alba Plena'. One of the first camellias to arrive in the West from China. The flowers are rather flat, medium-sized, formal double, white, with petals decreasing towards the centre. The habit is moderate in vigour and slightly open with small, light-coloured leaves.   ◐ **

'**Alba simplex**'. Raised in London in 1813, foliage from some of the old plants is still sold on the London markets for floristry work; it is dark green and glossy on a moderately vigorous, bushy plant. The flowers are flat, small to medium, single and white with occasional pink flecks. ◐ **

'**Alexander Hunter**'. An excellent Australian bred camellia. Named after its raiser, it first appeared in the Hazlewood nursery catalogue in 1941. A glowing red, medium-sized single flower with golden stamens, it is one of the first of the *japonica*s to bloom. It has a neat, upright, compact habit, with glossy leaves. ◐ **

The small-flowered *C. vernalis* varieties lend themselves to the controlled environment of a Japanese city

The massed display of camellias in the Eden Gardens, Auckland, are planted in a disused quarry

'**Ann Sothern**'. Bred in Sun Valley, California, it first flowered in 1954. The mid to late season flowers are semi-double with occasional petaloid stamens, 11-13cm across, and of an interesting creamy pale pink, becoming darker towards the petal tips. Although quite vigorous it forms a bushy upright plant with good glossy leaves. ◗

'**Annie Wylam**'. One of the author's favourites! From California (1960), it has medium-sized flowers mid to late season, bright pink shading to almost white at the centre, deep peony or rose form with many narow petals towards the centre. Attractive, deep, glossy green, pendant leaves on an upright slightly open bush. ◗ **

'**Apollo**' (**Pauls**). One of a group of seedlings produced by William Paul in about 1910. Sometimes confused with 'Jupiter', but 'Apollo' has deeper red flowers and a more open habit. Mid-season flowers are semi-double, with about 15 petals. Growth is tiered on a vigorous bush with long pointed leaves. ◗ **

'**Augusto Leal de Gouveia Pinto**'. From in Portugal in about 1904, it has white-edged petals which may be carmine, or on clay soils and/or in warm climates, lavender. Difficult to propagate by cuttings. ◗ **

'**Ave Maria**'. From San Jose, California, this camellia was registered in 1956. It has creamy pink formal double flowers of great purity and class, set off by broad dark green leaves. It blooms early to mid-season. ◗ **

'**Berenice Boddy**'. Named after the wife of the then publisher of the *Los Angeles Daily News*, in 1953. The flowers are semi-double, medium size and of a light peachy pink, with darker shading towards the base of the petals. It grows upright and vigorously, and is slightly open in habit, with a light appearance. One of the hardiest of all *japonica*s. ◗ ***

'**Betty Foy Sanders**' (1959). From Fred Smith in Georgia USA,. Named after the State Governor's wife, this prolific bloomer is a stable; white with strong irregular stripes on deep, medium-sized, deep, almost trumpet-shaped, semi-double flowers. Mid to late seasonon a compact, upright bush with wavy, dark green leaves. ◗ **

'**Betty Sheffield Supreme**'. A very striking but unstable sport of 'Betty Sheffield', found by Mrs Green Alday in Georgia, USA in 1956. The white semi-double flowers have distinct, deep pink petal margins. The leaves are oval, glossy, and mid-green on a moderately vigorous compact bush. ◗ **

'**Black Tie**'. Originated by Spencer Waldren Jr. in Georgia, USA in 1968, the flowers of this camellia are eminently suitable for corsages or button holes. They are small to medium, very dark red and very formal double, backed by neat dark green leaves. It flowers more freely in warm climates or under glass. Growth is of medium vigour and upright. ◗ **

'**Bob Hope**'. A must for every garden, it is tolerant of almost any conditions and very free flowering. Introduced by Nuccio's nursery in California in 1972, it has glowing red, irregular semi-double flowers mid-season to late. Its dark green, pointed leaves do not

The moongate at Eryldene, Sydney, is an interesting oriental feature amongst the camellias

damage easily and it has a compact, upright habit. ○ ◐ ● ***

'Bob's Tinsie'. Another Nuccio introduction, dating from 1962, this is a delightful little mid-season, is a bright red, anemone-form camellia. Growth is fairly slow and its branches slender, forming an upright compact bush. ◐ **

'Bokuhan' (sometimes known as 'Tinsie'). An old neat little, anemone-form Japanese camellia (1719), it has a dense convex mass of white petaloid stamens surrounded by bright red petals, early to mid-season. The finely toothed leaves are long, slender and dark green on an upright fairly vigorous bush. ◐ **

'Brushfield's Yellow'. First introduced in Australia by Camellia Grove nursery in 1970-71, it is almost identical in appearance to 'Gwenneth Morey' and to the *williamsii* hybrid 'Jury's Yellow'. White petals surround a mass of ruffled, pale primrose petaloids which, from a distance give the impression of yellow flowers on the bush in mid-season. Growth is bushy and upright. ◐ **

'C.M. Hovey'. (1850) Very easy, and still grown in most climates, it is vigorous and slightly open in habit, with large, glossy, deep green leaves. The flowers are large, regular formal double, rich crimson rose with the occasional white fleck. Early to mid-season. ◐● ***

'C.M. Wilson'. A sport of 'Elegans', first produced by Mrs A.E. Wilson of Florida and registered in 1949. This variety has large, anemone form flowers with silvery white outer petals shading to pink in the centre. Silvery white petaloids mix with golden stamens in the centre, which sometimes has strawberry red shades around it. The shallowly serrated, dark green, oval leaves sometimes twist and curl, and the bush is compact and slightly pendulous. ◑ **

'Cara Mia'. Introduced by Nuccio's nursery in their 1960/61 catalogue this high quality medium to large flowered semi-double is a beautiful blush pink shading to paler pink in the centre, where wavy petaloids mix with golden stamens. It is early to mid-season flowering on a vigorous upright bush. It is a little shy to bloom outdoors in cooler climates. ◑ **

'Carter's Sunburst'. (1951) Bred by E.H. Carter in California, the semi-double or peony-form or formal double flowers are medium to large pink striped deeper pink, and fairly stable. The foliage is mid to light green on a fairly vigorous rounded bush. ◑ ***

'Cherries Jubilee'. A 1983 introduction from Nuccio's nursery, the unusal flowers are semi-double or loose peony-form, with red and white petaloid stamens mixed with true yellow stamens. The bush is dense and upright, with long, narrow leaves, red-tinged when young. ◑ **

Lions and camellias go well together!

'**Commander Mulroy**'. Originated by T. Patin in Louisiana and registered in 1962, this durable variety survives because of the combination of beautiful, medium-sized formal double flowers which start off blush pink and age to pure white. They are set off by glossy dark green, rounded leaves on a tidy upright bush. Mid-season. ◐ **

Contessa Lavinia Maggi. See 'Lavinia Maggi'.

'**Dahlohnega**'. This was, for a short time, haled with some excitement as a yellow camellia when it first appeared in Georgia, USA, in 1983. It is not a true yellow but an attractive, soft creamy colour. The mid-season flowers are medium-sized, formal double, on an upright, slightly open bush of moderate to slow growth. ◐ **

'**Debutante**'. More famous as a parent of great merit than it is perhaps in its own right, it is, nonetheless, a lovely camellia which is one of the earliest *japonica*s to flower in spring. Its lovely medium-sized, soft 'powder' pink, very rounded, peony form flowers are surprisingly weather resistant. Growth is slow and the bush compact, which makes it ideal for small gardens. ◐ ***

'**Desire**'. (1977) A 'Dr Tinsley'crossing with 'Debutante' from David Feathers of Lafayette, California, this eye-catching camellia has medium to large formal, double flowers, pale pink, shading to darker pink towards the petal margins, early to late season. It produces 'rose bud' centres in warm conditions. Growth is vigorous, upright and fairly dense, with large dark green leaves.   ◐ **

'**Dixie Knight**'. Released in 1955 by the Central Georgia Nurseries, USA, this is popular in warm climates where its large, very deep red, semi-double or loose peony-form flowers are readily produced. The flower buds are large, oval, pointed at the base, and an attractive bronze/green, opening mid-season to late. Growth is vigorous, upright and compact. ◐ **

'**Dona Herzilia de Freitas Magalhaes**'. The camellia with the longest name, first listed in Portugal in 1949, its medium-sized, semi-double or sometimes anemone-form flowers may be purplish red, but on clay soils they are a distinctive violet colour. Growth is open and upright, blooms sparse. ◐ **

'**Donckelaeri**'. Verified as the correct spelling since the discovery of the signature of the head gardener of the Botanical Garden at Louvain in Belgium, after whom it was renamed in 1830 by Franz von Siebold from its original Japanese name of 'Masayoshi'. The flowers are mid-season, large, deep semi-double,and with strong notched petals which are red marbled white or white marbled red. The habit is bushy and upright with long, pointed leaves. ○ ◐ ***

'**Dr Burnside**'. Named after its originator from South Carolina, USA, and registered in 1962, this variety is made distinctive by the large robust bright yellow stamens which intermingle with the central petals in the rich red, usually peony-form flowers. Flowering season is mid-season to late, foliage is inclined to be pale unless plenty of nutrients are available. The bush grows dense and upright and is of moderate vigour. ◐ **

'Elegans'. Durable and famous in its own right and for its sports, it was bred 1823 by Alfred Chandler of Vauxhall, London. Not to be confused with the inferior 'Chandleri'. 'Elegans' has large anemone-form flowers in mid to late season. The listed description is 'rose opal with slightly darker venation', but 'salmon pink with rose' may be better. Occasional white blotches, due to virus, may appear. The leaves are broad, flat and serrated with pointed tips. ◐ ***

'Elegans Champagne'. A beautiful sport of 'Elegans' from the Nuccio's Nursery in 1977. It has large, waxy, white anemone-form flowers, sometimes with a very soft pink tinge at the base of the wavy edged petals and central petaloids. Disbudding is advisable to get good blooms. The leaves are more deeply serrated than 'Elegans', but otherwise of a similar habit. ◐ **

'Elegans Splendor'. Another 'Elegans' introduction from the Nuccio's nursery, but this time from 'C.M. Wilson', named in 1972. Both petals and leaves are markedly serrated and the petals are a soft pink shading to almost white at the wavy petal margins. Flowering time, habit and leaves are typically 'Elegans'. ◐ **

'Elegans Supreme'. Registered in 1960 as a mutant of 'Elegans', it is similar to its parent except that the flowers are a deeper colour, described as 'wine red', and with distinctly ruffled and wavy petals. ◐ **

'Elizabeth Weaver'. Originated by Dr Homeyer in Georgia USA in 1975, this beautiful coral pink large formal double, with its 138 petals, deserves to be more widely grown. It flowers early to mid-season and has medium slightly open upright growth. ◐ **

'Extravaganza'. This stunning camellia first appeared in the Nuccio's nursery catalogue in 1960 and has been attracting attention ever since. The mid season flowers are large to very large and deep, with broad anemone form centres, and with bold red and white stripes. The foliage is glossy green and the habit is upright and slightly open to give the flowers plenty of space. ◐

'Grand Prix'. Introduced in the Nuccio's nursery catalogue in 1968 it is both a consistent prize winner at shows and a marvellous landscape camellia. The large semi-double mid-season flowers are a brilliant glowing red, set off by bold, glossy dark green leaves on a vigorous spreading bush. ◐● **

'Guilio Nuccio'. Big, bold and stunning. The 12-15cm salmon red, mid-season, semi-double flowers are wide and deep, with wavy petals and usually some petaloids with prominent, mustard-coloured stamens in the centre. The bush grows big and broad, with strong textured glossy leaves. ◐ **

'Gwenneth Morey'. A chance seedling of 'Edith Linton', raised by Dr B.R. Morey, in New South Wales, Australia, this camellia was registered in 1963. It is very similar to 'Brushfields Yellow' and 'Jury's Yellow', with white petals surrounding a compact mass of primrose yellow petaloids, blooming in mid-season on an upright, bushy plant. ◐ **

'Hagoromo'. Most of us in the west know

this variety better as 'Magnoliiflora' or 'Magnoliaeflora', but as it is a very old Japanese cultivar and only imported into Italy and renamed as above in 1886, it has now been decided that it should be known under its original name. Its Italian name describes the beautiful, palest pink, medium-sized, hose-in-hose flowers, with their long, fluted petals very well. They are reminiscent of *Magnolia stellata*. Flowers are mid-season. Growth is compact and upright with narrow, pointed leaves. ◐● ***

'Happy Holidays'. First publicised in 1984, this camellia originated at the Nuccio's nursery. The blooms are large, pale pink, and formal double, on an upright bushy plant with neat dark green leaves, and is of moderate vigour. It has an exceptionally long flowering season, blooming early to late. ◐ **

"Hassaku-tsubaki' An old Japanese variety. It is a vermilion red single with good bright yellow stamens. The bush is slow growing, dense and mounded in habit, with deep glossy green leaves. It is early flowering and produces masses of blooms. ◐● **

'Hawaii'. A very attractive 'Elegans' variety, being a sport of C.M. Wilson, originated in 1954 by the Hamilton Clark nursery in California. The flowers are medium to large, palest pink, peony form and fimbriated at the petal margins. It is a very late blooming variety, with flowers sometimes found in mid-summer. ◐ **

'Holly Bright'. Introduced by the Nuccio's nursery in 1985, this is a different camellia. The mid-season flowers are large, semi-double, and light red, with a glowing crèpe texture. The leaves are broad and heavily serrated, giving a very holly-like appearance. Growth is compact, upright and fairly slow. ◐ **

'Janet Waterhouse'. Raised by E.G. Waterhouse in Australia and introduced in 1952, this neat, medium sized, pure white semi-double has beautiful golden stamens and it also weathers better than many white varieties. It blooms in mid-season. The leaves are small to medium size, dark green and borne on an upright bush of moderately dense habit. ◐ **

'Jupiter' (Paul, 1904). A useful light red single, with a prominent boss of stamens. It is hardier and more inclined to flower in cold northern areas than many *japonicas*. The blooms, which are mid-season, weather well too. Growth is upright and compact with glossy, dark green, fairly pointed leaves. ◐ ***

'Kathryn Funari'. This was originated in California by A. Funari in 1976 and has blooms which emerge early in the season. They are large, full formal double and a deep rosy pink, with prominent veining. The habit is vigorous and rather open. ◐ **

'Kewpie Doll'. A delightful little pale pink, mid-season, anemone-form miniature with a prominent raised central cluster of petaloids of the same colour. Growth is vigorous and upright, sometimes hiding and protecting, the flowers. It originated in 1971 in the McCaskill Gardens in Pasadena, California ◐ **

'Kick Off'. This striking peony form bi-colour first appeared in the Nuccio's catalogue in

1962. The large flowers are light pink with darker, rose pink stripes and flecks, blooming early to mid-season. The bush is compact upright and vigorous. ◐ **

'Konronkoku'. This is known by a variety of other names: 'Kouron Jura' and 'Nigra' being the most often used. It is an old Japanese variety with very dark red, medium-sized, rose form double flowers, with incurving petals, which are produced in great profusion from mid to late season. The habit is moderately vigorous and open and twiggy on a young bush, eventually forming a moderately vigorous, large, densely furnished bush with attractive, glossy green leaves. ◯◐ ***

'Kramer's Beauty'. Reckoned by many to be a much improved 'Kramer's Supreme', from which it is a chance seedling found at the Kramer Bros. Nursery in California and registered in 1981. The flowers are produced in great profusion, mid-season to late, medium to large, full peony form, and a 'vibrant red'. Like 'Kramer's Supreme', they have a very subtle, carnation-like perfume. Growth is vigorous, compact and upright. ◐ **

'Kuro-tsubaki'. The Black Camellia from Japan, which dates from 1829. Aptly named because the late season flowers, which emerge from dark red tinged buds, are of the deepest red. They have been variously described as double, open peony or semi-double. The petals are narrow and incurving, with irregular stamens. Most parts of the plant have a reddish tinge, including leaf petioles and young shoots. ◐ **

'Lady Clare'. See 'Akashigata'.

'Lady Loch'. A sport of the Australian bred 'Aspasia Macarthur'; it was first mentioned in Taylor and Sangster's catalogue in 1889, in Victoria, Australia. It is still widely grown, because its medium to large, light pink, peony form flowers are so attractive. They are veined darker pink, with paler margins, and are produced in mid-season. Growth is vigorous, upright and well spaced, with dark green leaves. ◐ **

'Lady Vansittart'. Originally from Japan, this was one of the 19th-century imports into Europe and arrived at the Caledonia nurseries, Guernsey, Channel Islands, via Belgium. It is one of the most unstable bi-colours, with mid-season, medium-sized, semi-double flowers, white streaked and blotched carmine rose, with petaloid stamens sometimes present amongst the central mass of golden yellow, fertile stamens. The leaves are long and fairly narrow, with finely, but sharply toothed margins. Its habit is compact and upright. ◯◐ ***

'Laurie Bray'. A favourite Australian variety, originated by George Linton in New South Wales and registered in 1955. It is a chance seedling, found under a bush of 'Edith Linton'. Its blooms are medium to large, semi-double, and of a lovely soft powdery pink, with even paler shading. The petals are well spaced and ruffled, with some petaloids amongst the stamens. The flowering season is medium to late, with masses of blooms, well displayed against a background of dark green leaves on an upright, quite vigorous bushy plant. A reliable and rewarding variety. ◐ **

'Lavinia Maggi'. More widely known as

'Contessa Lavinia Maggi', this variety was originally from Italy, but was introduced by the Van Houtte nursery in Belgium in 1858. The flowers are medium to large, formal double, with white petals striped carmine rose in mid-season. The foliage is bold on a dense mounded bush. 'Lavinia Maggi' sports readily to plain red (rosea) or white (alba). ◑ **

'Lemon Drop'. This delightful small to miniature camellia was originated by the Nuccio's nurseries in 1981. The blooms are anemone form and of a soft lemon colour, produced in mid-season. The leaves are dark green on a dense, upright bush of moderate vigour. ◑ **

'Lily Pons'. A very characterful camellia, registered in Oregon in 1955, and named after a famous opera singer of the day. The medium to large mid-season blooms are pure white, single or semi-double, with long narrow petals held stiffly around a central

boss of long stamens which have a greenish cast at the base. Growth is stiff and well spaced on an upright bush. ◑ **

'Lipstick'. Introduced by the Nuccio's nursery in 1981, this delightful small to miniature anemone form camellia has brilliant glossy red petals around a dense central mass of white petaloids bordered red. The mid-season flowers are produced in great profusion even on young plants; disbudding is advisable to encourage vegetative growth in the early years. The bush grows slowly and becomes dense and upright with small dark green leaves. ◑ **

'Little Bit'. This was originated by Dr John Lawson of California and registered in 1958. It is unlike any other camellia and can easily be mistaken, at first glance, for a carnation. It may either be plain red or more interestingly red with white flecking. The flowers are small, anemone form, with just five petals

'Lavinia Maggi' frequently sports plain red flowers

surrounding the central mass of petaloids. They bloom in mid-season on a vigorous, upright, rounded bush with attractive, smallish, rounded leaves. ◑ **

'Lovelight'. Originated by Harvey Short in California and introduced in 1962, this has to be one of the most beautiful camellias ever bred. Large, to very large semi-double pure white flowers, with golden stamens and strong textured petals, are produced from early/mid-season to late. They seem to weather incredibly well for their size and colour. The foliage is also superb; big bold leaves on a vigorous upright bush. ◑ **

'Magnoliiflora/Magnoliaeflora'. See 'Hagoromo'.

'Margaret Davis'. This Australian bred camellia appeared as a sport of 'Aspasia Macarthur' in the garden of its originator, A.M. Davis of New South Wales, in 1958

and still attracts the eye, especially at Camellia shows all over the world. The blooms are medium in size, peony form, with each raised, white petal edged deep carmine rose, forming a picotee flower of great charm and quality in mid-season. The foliage is bold, forming an upright, fairly vigorous bush.   ◑ **

'Man Size'. An odd name for a miniature. The anemone-form flowers are white with a mass of raised petaloids with some yellow stamens intermingled. It was introduced in 1961 and was originated by W.F. Wilson Jr. of Louisiana, USA, and has been winning prizes in classes for miniature blooms for many years. Its habit is upright, with paler than average leaves and with flowers rather sparsely produced. ◑ **

'Mark Alan'. Originated by Mr & Mrs Ashby from South Carolina, in 1957, this eye-catching camellia produces masses of large wine red-coloured peony form flowers, with

Bi-colour camellias.
Top left to right:
Margaret Davis. Nuccio's
Jewel, Tomorrow's Dawn
Bottom: Vittorio
Emanuel 2nd. Kick Off.
William Bartlett

distinctive, long, spoon-shaped petals, and petaloids interspersed with stamens in the centre. The blooms weather well and last a long time, making this an excellent landscape camellia. Growth is vigorous, forming a tall upright bush. ○◐ **

'Maroon and Gold'. Introduced in the Nuccio's catalogue in 1960 this small to medium variety always attracts attention because of the maroon colour of the petals, which surround the golden stamens of the peony form flowers which appear mid-season to late. It is a frequent winner on the show benches and is attractive as a garden plant because the leaves are exceptionally dark green and glossy on an upright bush. ◐ **

'Mars' (Paul 1911). Medium to large turkey red semi-double flowers with rather light textured petals and sometimes with white streaks, have attractive stamens in a central cylinder and bloom in mid-season. Its habit is spreading, forming attractive tiers, making this a useful variety for the front of a border. The leaves are dark green and fairly broad, with short pointed tips. ○◐ ***

'Matterhorn'. Raised by David Feathers of California and launched in 1981 by David Trehane in England, this medium-sized, mid-to-late season formal double is pure white and very full. The blooms shatter quickly in warm weather, but attract the attention of the judges on the show bench, and look stunning on the compact upright bush The handsome dark green, glossy leaves make a fine contrast. ◐ **

'Midnight Serenade'. First listed in the

Nucccio's nursery catalogue in 1973, this variety has bright red, medium-sized single blooms and is very free flowering over a long period, from early/mid-season to late. Its bushy, upright habit also makes it an excellent variety for a small garden or to grow in containers. ○◐● **

'Moonlight Bay'. From the Nuccio's nursery in 1982. This is one of the finest of their recent varieties. Although large to very large, its clear, pale orchid pink, semi-double flowers give an impression of simple elegance, both on the show bench and in a sheltered corner in the garden, in mid-season. Growth is vigorous, with dark green leaves, forming a large, upright, bushy plant. ◐ **

'Mrs D.W. Davis'. She has enormous very pale pink semi-double flowers with a few petaloid stamens amongst the golden fertile ones in the centre of the flower. These develop from big, fat, pointed buds and bloom in early to mid-sesaon. Petal texture is delicate so it is best kept under protection, otherwise the slightest knock or shower of rain causes bruising. The leaves are large and dark green on an upright, open bush. ◐ **

'Nigra' See 'Konronkoku'

'Nobilissima' apparently dates back to 1834, when it was raised by Lefèvre in Belgium, although there is still some dispute as some think it is an old Japanese variety introduced by Siebold in 1829 -1830 and renamed. It has a medium-sized, white, peony-formed flower which blooms early to mid-season on an open upright bush. The flowers damage very easily so it is best given some protection. ◐ **

'**Nuccio's Cameo**' was introduced into the family's catalogue in 1983. It has an exceptionally long flowering season, from early to late and has medium to large, coral rose/pink rose form or formal double flowers. Growth is dense, upright, and fairly slow, with neat, dark green leaves. ◐ **

'**Nuccio's Gem**'. One of the most beautiful formal double white camellias, especially when the pure white petals arrange themselves into a spiral. It was introduced in 1970 and continues to win on the show benches all over the world. It blooms in mid-season on an upright bushy plant with dark green, rather rounded leaves. Although it does well outdoors, even in cooler climates, its near perfect flowers deserve some protection. ◐ **

'**Nuccio's Jewel**'. Introduced in 1978, this showy camellia always attracts attention. The medium to large peony form blooms open mid-season to late and have great depth and a wonderful blending of palest and dark pink on the petals. Growth is slow to medium on an upright, bushy plant, with excellent dark glossy green leaves. The only problem is that, in Britain, the blooms do not weather well outside. It is a variety that is worth growing under protection. ◐ **

'**Nuccio's Pearl**' (1977). Similar in colouring to 'Nuccio's Jewel', but this is a medium sized mid-season to late formal double with good textured, slightly pointed petals, which somehow give it a certain air of purity, whereas 'Nuccio's Jewel' is more frothy and showy. The foliage is dark green and glossy on an upright, bushy plant of medium vigour. ◐ **

'**Okan**'. This is one of the most striking of the Higo camellias from the Kumamoto Prefecture of Japan, and was first publicised in a Japanese Camellia Society publication in 1982. The large, single flowers are pure white, with a very contrasting deep crimson edge to each petal. The stamens are typical 'Higo'; clearly arranged into a large cluster, with golden anthers. It is a mid to late blooming variety on an upright, fairly dense bush with good foliage. ◐ **

'**Patricia Ann**'. Registered in 1981 and originated by Howard Asper of California, this very large, very soft pink, mid season, camellia is a semi-double of great substance and depth, as well as size. It is not unlike one of its parents, 'Mrs D.W. Davis' in appearance, but the flowers weather better, probably because its other parent is the tough old favourite 'Berenice Boddy'. The large boss of central stamens has the occasional petaloid amongst them. Growth is upright and slightly open, with bold dark green leaves. ◐ **

'**Prima Ballerina**'. Introduced by the Nuccio's in 1987, this has a very broad, rather flat 'wide awake' flower of great quality and size, with wavy petals. It is pale pink at the centre, shading to darker pink towards the petal edges, with a wide cluster of loosely arranged stamens with the occasional petaloid amongst them. The flowering season is mid to late. The leaves are light green of moderate size, on a fairly vigorous bush. ◐ **

'**Princess Lavender**'. Originated in the USA in 1951, this is one of those varieties which is only worth growing where there is a high level of clay in the soil, as it then produces striking, rich, purple blooms. Otherwise they are just medium-sized, semi-doubles of an unremarkable deep red with lavender overtones. ◑ **

'Rubescans Major'. One of the classic French beauties from the 19th century and still appreciated today. The freely produced flowers are carmine pink and of a lovely regular formal shape, with masses of overlapping petals of robust texture. The centre of the flower sometimes reveals a few stamens when fully open in mid to late season. It forms an upright, dense, slow growing bush with fairly long leaves. ◑ ***

'Ruddigore'. One of the most rewarding red flowered camellias for landscape use. Bred by David Feathers in California, and introduced by David Trehane in 1980, it has masses of small to medium-sized, mid to late season blooms which are waxy red, semi-double and with intermingling stamens. The bush is upright, densely bushy and with attractive, bronze young growth. ○◑● ***

'San Dimas'. Another rewarding red camellia bred by another Californian, Clark Davis, and introduced in 1972. The flowers are large, semi-double, and a pleasing rich red, produced early to mid-season on an upright moderately vigorous plant. ◑ **

'Sawada's Dream'. This is an exquisite camellia, originated by K. Sawada of Alabama USA and introduced in 1959. The mid season to late flowers are medium to large, formal double, white in the centre gradually shading to pale pink towards the margins. When at its best the petals are arranged in a spiral.

C. sinensis 'Beni-bana-cha' is a delightful pink form of *C. sinensis*

Normally *C. sinensis* has small, pure white blooms

Growth is of medium vigour, slightly open in habit, with tough, finely toothed leaves. ◑ **

'Silver Anniversary'. Introduced by the Nuccio's nursery in 1960 its chief merit is in the commercial potential of its name. The flowers are semi-double, white, mid-season, and damage easily. The pale green leaves do not add to its attraction. ◑ **

'Silver Waves'. A much more attractive Nuccio introduction, with very large white semi-double mid-season flowers with wavy petals of good texture which withstand the weather quite well for a white. There are some wavy petaloids amongst the central, golden stamens. Growth is vigorous, slightly open and upright. ◑ **

'Something Beautiful'. This delightful miniature is aptly named. Originated by Edwin and June Atkins of Florida, and introduced in 1983 it has been winning classes for miniatures ever since. The flowers are formal double, pale pink, with a burgundy margin, on an upright bushy, vigorous plant.   ◑ **

'Tama-no-ura'. Said to have been discovered by a Japanes charcoal burner in 1947, growing wild , and introduced by the Nuccio's nursery in 1979, this attractive, small to medium-sized single camellia has just six rose-red petals, each edged white, with a cylinder of yellow stamens with white filaments. It blooms in early to mid-season, but rather sparsely in cooler areas.

A number of 'Tama' varieties have been produced by the Nuccio's nursery, which have not, at the time of writing, been properly assessed. They are 'Tama Americana', 'Tama Bambino', 'Tama Beauty', 'Tama Electra', 'Tama Glitters', 'Tama Vino'. All have white edges to their petals, but flower forms, sizes and base colours vary. ◑ **

'Taro'an'. A famous old Japanese variety, named after a famous devotee of the Tea Ceremony, for which this variety was much used. It has a pendulous habit and is best appreciated if planted on the top of a bank or wall where its lax branches can hang down and display its medium-sized, single pale pink, wide cup-shaped blooms to the best

advantage. It is one of the first *japonica*s to flower in the spring. ◑ **

'Tiffany'. A camellia which has won many awards since it first flowered in 1956, and still attracts the judges' attention. It was grown from Japanese seed imported into California. It has large, very deep, loose, peony-form flower of orchid pink, with slightly deeper shades, with just a few stamens amongst the twisted petals and petaloids. It flowers mid-season to late on an upright bush which can grow large. ◑ **

'Tinker Toy'. Originated by the Nuccio's nursery in 1981, this attractive anemone-form, mid- season miniature has both petals and petaloids of creamy white, flecked with red. Growth is bushy and moderately vigorous with rather light green leaves. The flowers keep their contrasting colours best if grown in fertile soil and in shade, otherwise they can be rather insipid. ◑ **

'Tom Thumb'. The mid-pink, formal double blooms have a blueish tinge with white borders to each pointed tipped petal. It blooms mid-season and is a little shy to start blooming as a young plant, but worth waiting for. It is of moderate vigour and upright. Introduced and originated by A. Kreuger of California. ◑ **

'Tomorrow'. This was originated by the Tick Tock nursery in Georgia, USA, and first bloomed in 1954. It has large peony form blooms of light red, in mid-season, produced somewhat sparsely on a vigorous bush of open, rather spreading habit. The leaves are oval, mid green and glossy. 'Tomorrow' has produced some outstanding sports. ◑ **

'Tomorrow Park Hill'. Actually a sport from a virus variegated form of 'Tomorrow', originated by Mrs Peer of Hollywood, California, and first publicised in 1964. It blooms in mid season, producing large to very large deep semi-double or loose peony-form flowers. 'Tomorrow Park Hill' can be distinguished from 'Tomorrow's Dawn' because it has soft pink petals shading to darker pink towards the petal edges. There are occasional white speckles due to virus. The habit is more upright than 'Tomorrow', but just as vigorous. ◑ **

'Tomorrow's Dawn'. This has very large flowers of loose peony form, similar to 'Tomorrow Park Hill' but with deep soft pink petals shading to paler pink at the centre. It also shades to white at the petal edges. The leaves and habit are similar to its parent, 'Tomorrow', from which it sported in Mississippi, and was first publicised in the *American Year Book* in 1960. ◑ **

'Ville de Nantes'. First mentioned in 1897, and published in the *Guichard Soeurs* catalogue in 1920, this very individual camellia is still popular despite the fact that its variegation is due to virus. The large, deep, frilly flowers are semi-double, deep red with blotches and streaks of white, and with finely toothed petal margins. Leaves are dark green, glossy and long, but often with yellow marbling due to virus. There is also a plain red form. ◑ **

'White Nun'. Bred by McCaskill in California and introduced in the *American Yearbook* in 1959, this camellia has very large, semi-

double blooms with robust, pure white petals and a central boss of golden stamens. The bush is vigorous, upright and rounded with dark green foliage. ◑ **

'Wilamina'. A delightful, very free flowering variety, producing masses of formal double soft pink blooms, with a subtle paler margin to the petals which curve gently inward. Growth is slow, forming a bushy, narrow, upright plant, ideal for small gardens. Its originator was C.A. Pederson of California, and it was first publicised in 1951. ○◑● **

'Wildfire'. A 1963 introduction from the Nuccio's nursery. It has bright orange/red semi-double flowers with a tubular boss of yellow stamens and flowers mid-season. Petal texture is a little light so protection is needed in adverse conditions. The foliage is dark green on an upright fairly vigorous bush. ◑ **

'William Bartlett'. (1958). Found by William Bartlett of New South Wales, as a seedling growing under a bush of 'Mrs Scottowe'. The flowers are a full formal double, large, pale pink with masses of darker pink stripes and flecks, making this a very attractive, subtle, stable bi-colour for those who find many bi-colours too gaudy and unstable. ◑

'Yours Truly'. This first appeared in the Fruitland nursery catalogue in Georgia, USA in 1947. It is an enduring sport of Lady Vansittart, with pale pink, semi-double flowers veined deeper pink and shading to white at the petal tips. The foliage is a little broader than its parent but it is otherwise similar in habit. ◑ **

SOME *WILLIAMSII* VARIETIES

These are all hybrids between *C. saluenensis* and varieties of *C. japonica* or are second generation, with the *saluenensis* parent being itself a *williamsii*. Most, but not all of them, have small, tough leaves, inherited from *C. saluenensis,* which have matt rather than shiny surfaces.

'Anticipation'. (*C. saluenensis* x*C*. j. 'Leviathan'). The large peony form, rich rose pink/red flowers of this outstanding camellia, freely produced on a fairly narrow, bushy, upright plant, make this an excellent variety both for landscape use and for shows. Its long, glossy leaves are attractive too. Flowering season is early to late, but the earliest blooms are sometimes poor in quality. 'Anticipation', like so many *williamsii* varieties, was bred by New Zealand hybridist Les Jury and first flowered in 1959. ○◐● ***

'Anticipation' variegated. The white spots and blotches are due to virus, which has been deliberately induced. Not for the purist but it is an eye-catching camellia which wins countless prizes on the show benches.

'Ballet Queen' (1976). A sister seedling of 'Anticipation', from Les Jury, but with lighter pink flowers which bloom a little later. ○◐● ***

'Blue Danube'. A relatively slow growing, compact bush, with paeony form, occasionally semi-double, medium-size blooms which are rose pink with violet tones. Mid-season. Introduced by the McCaskill Gardens, California, in 1960. ○◐● **

'Bow Bells' (1954). One of the most valuable camellias for cold climates as it flowers from early to late and the blooms are very weather resistant. The flowers are medium-sized, mid-pink, trumpet shaped, semi-doubles and very prolific. The habit is upright, with fine twiggy growth which becomes attractively pendulous with age. The leaves are small and matt. Bred by Jimmy Marchant of England. ○◐● ***

'Bridal Gown'. A variable camellia, being formal double for its raiser, David Feathers, in California, but full peony, like its *japonica* parent, 'Debutante' when grown in England by its introducer, David Trehane. The white flowers are medium-sized, mid-to-late season on an upright bush with mid-green leaves with prominent veining. ◐● ***

'Brigadoon'. Much loved by all who grow it, this is an exceptionally hardy, beautiful camellia, with its mid to deep pink semi-double flowers borne on a robust, upright, slightly open bush. The leaves are strong in texture. ○◐● ***

'Buttons 'n Bows'. This first appeared in the Nuccio's nursery catalogue in 1985. It has an interesting small formal double flower, pale pink, shading to darker at the petal margins. The petals are curved and fluted. The bush grows very slowly, takes time to get established, and is very dense and bushy. Good for a small garden where the owner has patience. ◐● **

'Charity' (*C. saluenensis* x *C.j.* 'Waiwhetu Beauty' 1975). Bred by Les Jury in New Zealand. The medium to large semi double flowers are a bright pink with blue undertones and are mid to late season on a fairly vigorous, spreading bush with glossy leaves. It is a very weather-resistant variety. ○◑● ***

'**Charles Colbert**' (chance seedling from seed collected from *C. saluenensis*)(1959). Originated by Professor Waterhouse in Australia this is an upright camellia which carries masses of medium-sized, clear pink, semi-double flowers, which drop cleanly when spent, on a neat upright bush. ○◑● ***

'**Charles Michael**'. One of the classic *williamsii* hybrids, having the largest flowers of the series, but bred by Julian Williams, son of John C. at Caerhays Castle in Cornwall, England. Flowers are medium, single, with fairly long petals with the inner row very pale pink and the outer rows a darker clear pink. Growth is vigorous, open and upright, with leaves which are larger and glossier than most *williamsii* varieties. ○◑● ***

'**China Clay**'. Bred by Gillian Carlyon in Cornwall, England where the china clay pits are a prominent feature, and introduced in 1973, this is an aptly named pure white, semi-double camellia. 'J.C. Williams' xC.j. 'Marjorie Magnificent'. Mid-season. The habit is open, spreading and fairly vigorous with mid green leaves. ◑● **

'**Citation**'. (1958). Its origins are uncertain, but it was first distributed by Bodnant gardens in Wales. One of the palest pink blooms, semi-double, medium-sized and prolifically produced on a vigorous, upright bush. ◑● **

'**Contribution**'. A 'Donation' seedling raised by David Feathers in California and introduced by David Trehane in England in 1991. This is a particularly slow growing and compact variety, reaching about one metre in 12 years. The semi-double flowers are mid-pink, a little deeper in colour than 'Donation', with a slightly fuller flower, and produced in great profusion from mid to late season. It is ideal for the front of a border or in small gardens, and, like its parent, is tolerant of heavy shade. ○◑● **

'**Coral Delight**'. Introduced by Kramer Bros Nursery in California in 1975 this is a C. *japonica* 'Dr Tinsley' x *C. saluenensis* semi-double, medium-sized hybrid, with two rows of strong, textured petals of glowing coral with the occasional white fleck. It is mid to late season blooming on an upright bushy plant. ○◑● **

'**Debbie**' (*C. saluenensis* x *C.j.* 'Debutante') One of the most widely grown *williamsii*, probably because it is so easy to propagate and grow. It is a vigorous, upright grower, producing masses of very bright, almost shocking pink, medium-sized, peony-form flowers from early to late. The leaves tend to be pale green unless nutrients are supplied in abundance. Bred by Les Jury in New Zealand and introduced in 1966. ◑● ***

'**Debbie's Carnation**'. Bred by Felix Jury and of the same parentage as 'Debbie' this seedling first flowered in 1971. It is similar to 'Debbie' but better in every way, more compact in habit, darker green leaves, bigger flowers, which seem to weather even better than its sister seedling. ○◑● ***

'**Donation**'. Bred by Col. Stephenson Clarke in Surrey and first publicised in 1941, this is the most widely grown of all *williamsii*, and deservedly so. It does best in cooler climates, where it can be relied upon to bloom freely year after year from mid-season to late. It is prone to die back (*Botrytis*) in hotter humid areas. The medium to large semi-double flowers are orchid pink with darker veining. It grows upright to form a tall, wide bush with small, robust leaves. ○◐● ***

'**Dream boat**' (*C. saluenensis* x C.j. 'K. Sawada'). Originated by Felix Jury in 1976. This has large, very beautiful very full formal double flowers with incurving petal margins. The colour is a good bright, but not garish, pink. Mid-season. Growth is vigorous, forming an open upright bush, with larger leaves than most *williamsii* hybrids. Needs to be kept under control with secateurs. ○◐● **

'**E.T.R. Carlyon**'. ('J.C. Williams' x 'Adolphe Audusson'). Bred by Gillian Carlyon in Cornwall and introduced in 1972, this medium-sized, semi-double or sometimes double white camellia blooms mid to late season. Growth is upright and fairly vigorous with pale foliage. ◐● **

'**E.G. Waterhouse**'. Named after its breeder in Australia in 1946 this beautiful, formal double pink is late flowering on an upright bush with rigid, well spaced branches. The flowers shatter rather quickly. ○◐● **

'**Elegant Beauty**' (*C. saluenensis* x C.j. 'Elegans'). Bred by Les Jury in New Zealand this produces medium to large, deep rose-pink flowers which may be anemone form, peony form or semi-double on the same bush at the same time. Mid-season to late. Its habit is open with vigorous growth which is an attractive bronze when young, becoming dark green later. The leaves are larger and more glossy than most *williamsii* hybrids. ○◐● ***

'Contribution' is extremely compact and ideal for the front of a shady border

'**Elsie Jury**'. Another introduction from Les Jury, New Zealand, in 1964. Bred from *C. saluenensis* x C.J. 'Pukekura', it has large, very full, soft pink, peony-form flowers, produced from large, rounded buds which open mid to late season. The foliage is broader and glossier than most *williamsii* hybrids, on an open, vigorous upright bush with strong branches. ◐◑ **

'**Francis Hanger**' (C.j. 'Alba Simplex' x *C. saluenensis*). Bred at the RHS Gardens at Wisely, England, by Francis Hanger in 1946. It has nine bery pure white petals with a contrasting cylindrical boss of golden stamens, forming a medium-sized flower. It is slow growing forming a fairly low, compact bush. ◑● **

'**Freedom Bell**'. This is from Nuccio's Nursery, California and is of unknown parentage, but is thought to be a *C. japonica* x *C. saluenensis* cross. It has light red, small, semi-double, bell-shaped flowers produced in abundance in early to mid season, even in cold areas. Growth is upright, twiggy, and open to start with, later forming a dense upright bush with typical *williamsii* leaves. ◑● ***

'**Galaxie**' 1996. Bred in California, this is a medium-sized rose form or formal double, wihich often forms a 'rosebud' centre in warm weather. It is basically a very pale pink with very subtle darker pink stripes. The flowering season is mid to late on an upright bush of medium vigour. ◑● **

'**Garden Glory**' first bloomed in 1968 and was released in 1974 by the Nuccio's Nursery in California. It is one of the earliest to flower

The 'Donation' seedling 'Contribution' has the same attractive veining as its parent

'Garden Glory'

and its beautiful, medium-sized, rich orchid pink, rose-form double flowers are not produced until late in spring. They weather exceptionally well. Growth is moderate, forming an upright, rounded bush, with slightly glossy, larger than usual leaves. ◯◑● ***

'**Gay Time**'. (*C. saluenensis* x C.j. 'Julia Drayton'). This was bred by Les Jury in New Zealand and released by Nuccio's Nursery in

'Joan Trehane' may have peony-form and rose-form double flowers on the same bush in warm conditions

1973. It is popular in London. The pale pink, irregular, semi-double flowers are large and mid-season, produced in profusion on a rounded, bushy plant. ◑● **

'J.C. Williams' (*C. saluenensis* x *C. japonica*). Masses of pale pink flowers are produced from early to late season. They are single and small to medium-sized of pale pink shading to darker pink, with golden stamens in the centre. The bush is slow growing, eventually forming a big plant as tall as it is wide. The leaves are typical *williamsii*. ○◑● ***

'Joan Trehane' (*C. saluenensis* x C.j 'Hikarugenji', 1979). Bred by Les Jury in New Zealand and named after the author's mother, this beautiful late to very late blooming camellia normally has rose form, double flowers in most British seasons, but may produce loose peony-form blooms in warmer

than usual conditions. The flowers are medium to large and of a clear rose pink. The bush is vigorous and open in habit. ○◑● ***

'Jury's Yellow'. (*C. saluenensis* x C.j. 'Daikagura' x C.j. 'Gwenneth Morey'). Bred by Les Jury in New Zealand. First flowered in 1971. Very like 'Gwenneth Morey' and 'Brushfields Yellow', being a medium-sized anemone-form flower with nine white petals and a mass of creamy yellow petaloids. Mid season. Growth is upright and bushy, with light green leaves. 'Jury's Yellow' is one of those varieties which can be shy to flower, but if moved even a metre away, it will often bloom regularly from then on. ◑● **

'Mary Phoebe Taylor'. Registered in New Zealand in 1975 and raised by J. Taylor. The light, slightly rosy pink, peony form or semi-double flowers are large to very large and very freely produced mid-season to late on a vigorous, upright, spreading bush. It is a wonderful variety for showing or landscape use in Britain and similar climates. Leaves are long and narrow, glossier than most *williamsii*. It seems to be happy in most situations, even in full sun. ○◑● ***

'Muskoka'. This English raised variety first appeared in the *Crown Estates* catalogue, Windsor, in 1979. There is an excess of pink semi-double *williamsii* hybrids available, but this one is one of the best. The pink is rich and clear, the flowers medium-sized, and cover the bush from mid-season to late, dropping as they age to form a colourful carpet, The foliage is deep green and attractive on an upright, tidy, fairly vigorous bush. ○◑● ***

'Pink Dahlia'. (1981). Originated by the Kramer Bros Nurseries in California, this is an unusual camellia, with flowers small in size, of a lavender pink, double or rose-form double. The petals are narrow and pointed, giving a dahlia-like appearance. Mid-season. The leaves are also narrow and growth upright, rather stiff and open. Plants may take time to get established. ◐ **

'Rose Parade'. Introduced by the Nuccio's Nursery in 1969, 'Rose Parade' has proved to be very hardy, with beautiful rose red formal double blooms which bloom mid-season to late in cool climates. It is a 'Donation' x *C. japonica* hybrid. The bush has well spaced, rigid branches with broad leaves for a *williamsii* and is fairly vigorous. ○◐● ***

'Senorita'. Of the same parentage as 'Joan Trehane', (*C. saluenensis* x C.j. 'Hikarugenji'). Bred by Les Jury in New Zealand, first flowered in 1957, this is one of Les Jury's best camellias. It has gorgeous medium-sized flowers, deep semi-double or peony form, very frilly (like flamenco dancers' dresses) and bright pink. They are very freely produced from mid to late season on a bushy, fairly vigorous, upright bush with good, glossy, dark green leaves. ◐● ***

'St Ewe' (Caerhays, Cornwall, 1947). A very reliable, easy to grow camellia, with rose pink, single, trumpet flowers similar to 'Bow Bells' but slightly deeper pink and a little larger. It flowers early to late for a slightly shorter period than 'Bow Bells'. Its habit is upright, bushy and vigorous, with glossy leaves. ○◐● ***

'Tiptoe'. Registered in Australia in 1965, it originated at Camellia Grove Nursery, St Ives, NSW. It is very floriferous, with mid to late season medium-sized, semi-double flowers of a lovely soft pink, deepening to a darker pink at the petal tips. Growth is slow, upright and very bushy, making this an ideal variety for hedging or for tubs. ○◐● **

'Water lily' (*C. saluenensis* x C.j. 'K. Sawada' 1967). Bred by Felix Jury, this beautiful medium to large very full formal double looks just like a pink water lily. It blooms mid-season to late, on an upright bush which tends to be undisciplined and to need regular pruning to start with. The leaves are glossy and dark green. ○◐ **

'Wilber Foss' (*C. saluenensis* x C.j. 'Beau Harp'). Another Les Jury variety from New Zealand, registered in 1975. It has large, deep, peony-form flowers of deep claret red, mid to late season, on an upright compact plant of moderate vigour. Leaves are glossy and similar to those of 'Anticipation'. ○◐● **

'Wynne Rayner'. From B.J. Rayner of New Zealand, this is very similar to 'Mary Phoebe Taylor', but has slightly deeper pink flowers and a more compact habit. It performs well in hot climates. ○◐ **

LARGE-FLOWERED *CAMELLIA RETICULATA* CULTIVARS AND HYBRIDS

These include some of the original 'Yunnan' *reticulata* cultivars and hybrids sent from Kunming, and other, more recent varieties whcih have *C. reticulata* in their parentage. All are obtainable from specialist camellia nurseries, but some may take some seeking out.

'Arch of Triumph'. This first bloomed in 1962 for its originator, David Feathers, in California. The flowers, produced early in the season, are large to very large, up to 17cm across and 8cm deep, of a loose, peony form and wine red with yellow stamens. Growth is upright, vigorous and more bushy than most *reticulata*s. ○◑ **

'Buddha'. Included in the original consignment of *reticulata*s sent from Kunming, China, to the Descanso Gardens in California as a seedling. It is a hybrid between an unknown *C. reticulata* and *C. pitardii* var *yunnanica*. The flowers are deep pink with irregular, upright, wavy petals and its habit is vigorous and upright. Mid-season. ○◑ **

'Captain Rawes'. Certainly the oldest, most established *reticulata* cultivar in Britain. The large to very large (up to 17cm across), semi-double or loose peony form flowers are a bright rose madder, paler towards the centre, early to mid-season. Growth, once established is vigorous, open and upright, forming a small tree, with rather matt leaves. This variety is regarded as difficult to propagate and is usually grafted. ○◑ **

'Curtain Call'. Introduced by the Nuccio's Nursery in 1979, its parentage is unknown. The flowers are very large, deep coral rose, semi-double with fluted petals, and of show winning qualtiy. Growth is open, upright and vigorous, with large light green leaves. ○◑ *

'Debut'. Another Nuccio introduction, this *C. reticulata* x *C. japonica* cultivar was introduced in 1977. It has very large, showy, loose peony-form flowers, which bloom mid-season. 'Debut' has glorious rose red, wavy petals. Growth is upright and rapid, but denser than most *reticulata* hybrids. ○◑ **

'Dr Clifford Parks'. This was originated in North Carolina by Dr Clifford Parks and is a hybrid between one of the original Kunming *reticulata*s, 'Daraohong' – synonym 'Crimson Robe' – and the red *C. japonica* 'Kramer's Supreme' and is probably the most popular of all the large-flowered *reticulata*s, with many awards to its credit. Its very large, mid-season flowers are anemone or peony form, red, with an orange cast on young blooms, which is lost as they age. Growth is vigorous, upright and compact. ○◑ **

'Francie. L'. Originally from the Huntington Gardens, California, this is a cross between *C. saluenensis* 'Apple Blossom' and *reticulata*s 'Buddha' and has large to very large, semi-double mid-season flowers, with waxy petals which are more light salmon red than the officially described rose pink. The leaves are distinctive, narrow, and, especially in cold climates, leathery and almost strap-shaped. Growth is strong, vigorous and open, making this an ideal variety for training on walls. It has also done well after some of the more severe British winters. ○◑● **

'Harold L. Paige'. The large, bright red, late flowers of this *reticulata* hybrid are rose-form double or sometimes full peony and of robust texture, often forming crowded multiple flower heads unless some of the buds are thinned. It is a hybrid between C.j 'Adolphe Audusson' and *C. reticulata*

'Dataohong' ('Crimson Robe') introduced in 1969 in California. Growth is strong, upright and reasonably compact for a *reticulata*. ◯◖ **

'Lasca Beauty'. *C. reticulata* 'Damanao' ('Cornelian') x *C. japonica* 'Mrs D.W. Davis' produced this large, elegant, mid-season blooming, soft pink, semi-double, displayed so well against its broad, dark green leaves. It originated from Dr Clifford Parks and first bloomed in 1970 while he was working at the L.A.S.C.A. (Los Angeles State County Arboretum). It forms a large, open upright bush with robust growth. ◯◖ **

'Miss Tulare'. A large to very large, brilliant, rose red *reticulata* with flowers of great depth, being either full peony or rose-form double. It first bloomed in California in 1973. It is an open-pollinated seedling of 'Dataohong'. Growth is vigorous and upright. ◯◖ **

'Nuccio's Ruby'. Of unknown parentage, this is one of the richest reds, with ruffled, semi-double blooms, flowering in mid-season on upright, dense bush of medium vigour. ◯◖ **

'Otto Hopfer'. *C. x reticulata* 'Crimson Rose' x *C. japonica* 'Lotus' originated by D. Hopfer of San Francisco in 1972. Large and very clear light red semi-double with irregular petals. Vigorous upright growth. Mid-season flowering. ◯◖ **

'Overture'. An Australian bred mid-season *reticulata* (F.S. Tuckfield, 1970) of great quality, this camellia has large to very large,

almost luminescent, rose red of deep pink semi-double flowers with upstanding wavy petals many of which curve back to form loose tubes. It is another chance seedling from 'Dataohong'. Growth is vigorous but compact. ◯◖ **

'Pagoda' see 'Songzilin'.

'Red Crystal'. Bred by Oz Blumhardt in New Zealand from *C. reticulata* 'Dataohong' x *C. japonica* 'Wildfire' and introduced in 1984, this is an eye-catching brilliant scarlet red, with large semi-double or single flowers, sometimes with as few as four very large, very robust petals wtih a glowing, heavy waxy texture. The foliage is an attractive dark green, on a bushy, upright plant. ◯◖ **

'Robert Fortune'. See 'Songzilin'.

'Royalty'. Bred in California by T.E. Croson and introduced in 1970, this reliable *reticulata* has large light rose red, ruffled, semi-double flowers which are deper red in the centre. It is a result of a cross between *C. japonica* 'Clarise Carlton' and *C. reticulata* 'Zhangia Cha' ('Chang's Temple'), and blooms mid to late season. ◯◖● **

'Songzilin'. Robert Fortune bought this *reticulata* to England in the 19th century, when it was named 'Reticulata Flore Plena', and it has also been known by the English translation, 'Pine Cone', of its correct Chinese name, given because the outer petals look like the scales of a pine cone as they first open. The flowers are deep pink, formal double, with petals arranged in whorls. It is difficult to obtain mainly because it is hard to propagate

The *reticulata* hybrid 'Red Crystal' has very large, very robust blooms and looks promising for outdoor cultivation in the southern half of Britain

'Valentine Day' is a *reticulata* hybrid with enormous flowers

and to grow as a young plant. ○◐ **

'Valentine Day'. This is an outstanding camellia, which produces masses of large or very large blooms on a strong bush with excellent leaves. The flowers are very full formal double, with so many petals that the centre seems to be pushed upwards, or to form a rosebud centre. The colour is medium salmon pink, with lighter tones as the flowers age. 'Valentine Day' was bred by Howard Asper in California from 'Dataohong' ('Crimson Robe') x *C. japonica* 'Tiffany'. ○◐ **

'White Retic'. This very pale pink does not quite match its name. It is a *C. reticulata* x *C. japonica* hybrid of unknown parentage, introduced by the Nuccio's Nursery in 1979. Of vigorous upright growth in California, for some reason it does not thrive even under glass in Britain. ○◐ **

THE *SANSANQUAS*

(This includes *C. hiemalis* and *C. vernalis* cultivars)
This is just a very small selection. Those living in hot climates will find many more in the catalogues of specialist nurseries in their areas.

'Bert Jones'. This came from Camellia Grove nursery in St Ives, New South Wales, in 1958 and its parentage is unknown. The broad leaves are larger than most *sasanquas* as are also the flowers which are semi-double and of a lovely soft silvery pink. It blooms very early on an upright bush . ◐ **

'Bonanza' (*C. x hiemalis*). This showy camellia originated in Alabama, from Tom Dodd Jr. in

1962. It has medium-sized, deep red semi-double or peony form flowers with yellow stamens, very early, on a vigorous bush with attractive dark green leaves. ○◐ **

'Crimson King'. Probably the most frequently grown sasanqua in Britain in the past because it has more robust petal texture and flowers more freely than many others. It is a large to medium-sized, semi-double, deep crimson with golden stamens flowering in autumn/winter. It originated in Japan and was first publicised in 1937. ○◐ **

'Dazzler' (*C. hiemalis*). A very apt name for a very bright rose red flower. It is small to medium-sized and flowers in mid-autumn/winter. It forms an open bush which is ideal for training. ◐ **

'Gay Border'. Introduced in 1986 by the Thermal Nurseries in Roturua, New Zealand, for its breeder, Jack Clark, this is a striking, large, single or semi-double with white or very pale pink petals, heavily shaded rose red. ○◐ **

'Gay Sue'. The frilly, white petals and cream anthers of the small to medium-sized flowers give this *sasanqua* an individuality. It originated from Trevor Lennard in New Zealand, and is of upright, dense habit ○◐ **

'Hiryu' (*C. vernalis*). Also incorrectly called 'Kanjiro', particularly in Australia. Like many vernalis cultivars it is quite cold-hardy and blooms late in the winter, into early spring, on an upright, bushy plant with attractive dark green leaves. The flowers are small, deep rose red and with jumbled petals. ○◐ **

'**Hugh Evans**'. One of the first *sasanqua*s to flower in early autumn, it is a small single, with deep rose pink petals on a vigorous, upright bush with small, neat leaves. From the Coolidge Rare Plant Gardens in California and was raised from seed imported from Japan. ○◖ **

'**Jean May**'. Originated by Ralph May in Florida this *sasanqua* was raised from seed of unknown parentage and publicised by the Southern California Camellia Society in 1951. It has become popular all over the world ever since. The flowers are medium-sized, double, blush to shell pink, deeper towards the centre shading to almost white at the petal edges. Long and narrow petals, with the outer ones notched at the margins. It is vigorous, forming an upright bush. ○◖ **

'**Jennifer Susan**'. A popular *sasanqua* in Australia where it was originated by Dr Ducker and registered in 1963. It has small to medium, pale pink, peony-form flowers with curled petals, in early autumn. It is an upright, slow grower. ○◖ **

'**Mignonne**'. Introduced from Professor Waterhouse's garden in 1979 this has miniature, formal, double light pink flowers in mid autumn on a bushy upright plant. ○◖ **

'**Narumigata**'. Originated in the Kanto district of Japan in 1898 this camellia is also regrettably sold as *Camellia oleifera* and vice versa. The flowers are similar, both being single, large, cup-shaped and white. The forms of *C. oleifera* in commercial circulation may have just a hint of magenta at the tips of some petals while 'Narumigata' has more.

'Narumigata' also flowers later, from late autumn to mid-winter in Britain. ○◖ **

'**Navajo**'. This is a very eye-catching camellia, with its semi-double medium-sized blooms with their white flowers and very pronounced rose red borders. It forms a bushy upright plant. Although the variety originally came from Japan and originally had a Japanese name, it was renamed and later distributed by the Nuccio's nurseries in California, after first being publicised by Wylam in 1956. ○◖ **

'**Nodami-ushiro**'. This *sasanqua* was imported into California from Japan about 1934 by the Domoto nursery. It has medium-sized, rose pink, single to semi-double flowers on an upright, fairly dense bush of some vigour. It flowers early, (one of the first of the *sasanqua*s to bloom), and freely. ○◖ **

'**Paradise Belinda**'. First available in 1995, this is one of the most showy of the new *sasanqua*s bred by Bob Cherry in New South Wales, with its large, 11cm, flat, glowing pink semi-double flowers. They are borne over a long season from early to late autumn on a dense, compact bush with dark green leaves. ○◖ **

'**Paradise Blush**'. First sold in Australia in 1992, this is a very useful bushy upright *sasanqua* with deep pink flower buds which open to small white flowers with pink on the under side of the outer petals. The mature foliage is dark, glossy green with new growth an attractive reddish colour. ○◖ **

'**Paradise Little Liane**'. A mass of small, white, loose, peony form blooms on a dense bush with tiny leaves makes this one of the best varieties for growing in pots or for topiary and low hedging. It makes a good, low standard too. Introduced in 1994. ○◑ **

'Paradise Petite'. A 1995 introduction, this is one of the most attractive of *sasanqua*s, with a very appropriate name. It is very compact and slow growing, ideal for containers and for topiary and low hedging. The lovely small flowers are soft pink, loose peony form with an attractive ruffled appearance, produced in abundance. ○◑ **

'Paradise Sayaka'. This 1997 introduction promises to be one of the most popular of Bob Cherry's *sasanqua*s, with its profusion of flowers produced over a long period . They are semi-double or loose peony with pink buds opening to white, with a soft pink border. With many flowers all at different stages of pink and white on a tall narrow bush, with long dark green leaves, this is a most attractive variety. ○◑ **

'Plantation Pink'. Originated by Professor Waterhouse in Australia and first sold through the *Camellia Grove* catalogue in 1948, this camellia is well known throughout the world. Its medium, soft pink, saucer-shaped, single flowers are well displayed against the small, dark green leaves. Its habit is pendulous and spreading. The texture of both leaves and flowers is light and it does not like damp conditions in winter. ◑ *

'Shishigashira' (*C. hiemalis*). There are several forms of this variety, one being a lighter pink and another a tall growing form with pale pink flowers. The original is a medium sized

bright rose red semi-double or loose, peony-form very free flowering on a low growing rather sprawling bush which is ideal for training. It is seen as a trained container plant in urban areas all over Japan. ○◑ ***

'Sparkling Burgundy'. Issued with a plant patent in 1959, this Louisiana bred camellia is popular world wide. It forms an upright, slightly spreading bush with dark green leaves. The flowers are described as 'Rose Bengal' but rosy pink would possibly be more realistic. They are peony form, almost anemone form, and produced over a long season from mid-autumn into winter. ◑ **

'Star Above Star' (*C.vernalis*). From the McCaskill Gardens in California, in 1964, this is a really unusual camellia. The flowers are semi-doubles in the form of one star imposed upon another, white in the centre, shading to pink at the edges of the long, fluted petals. Its habit is vigorous, upright and bushy. ○◑ **

'Tanya'. A very slow, low growing camellia with small leaves and masses of small, single, deep rose-pink flowers produced in mid-autumn. This is an ideal variety for the front of a sunny border or for pot growing. ○◑ **

'Yuletide' (*C. vernalis*). Most aptly named and very hardy. (The author has seen blooms withstand -6ºC undamaged), the flowers, which are produced in profusion over a long period from mid-winter to early spring, are brilliant red, with golden stamens. The bush is upright and dense, with very dark green leaves. Introduced by the Nuccio's Nurseries in 1963. ○◑ **

A plateful of 'Paradise' *sasanqua*s at the home of their breeder Bob Cherry in Australia

Bushy upright: 'Gay Sue', 'Hugh Evans, 'Jean May', 'Navajo', 'Paradise Blush', 'Paradise Pearl', 'Paradise Sakaya', 'Star above Star', 'Yuletide'.
Open upright: 'Bert Jones', 'Jennifer Susan', 'Narumigata', 'Plantation Pink'.
Rounded, bushy: 'Crimson King', 'Paradise Belinda'.

Bushy, fairly low growing: 'Bonanza', 'Crimson King', 'Sparkling Burgundy'.
Dwarf, small-leaved: 'Paradise Little Lianne', 'Paradise Petite', 'Tanya'.

HYBRIDS OTHER THAN *WILLIAMSII* OR LARGE FLOWERED *RETICULATA* HYBRIDS

'Alpen Glo'. As a chance seedling of 'Snowdrop', this camellia has *C. pitardii* and

C. fraterna in its make-up, and has gradually become appreciated across the world since its introduction in 1985 by Edgar Sebire in Victoria, Australia. It has miniature single or semi-double flowers which are pale pink shading to darker pink towards the edges. It is very free flowering, with flowers along the branches, and proving, to date, hardy for southern England. It has slender arching growth, with grey-green leaves inherited from *fraterna*. It grows well in full sun in England, but prefers semi-shade in hotter climates. ◖ *

'Baby Bear' *C. rosiiflora* x *C. tsaii*. Bred by Neville Haydon and introduced in New Zealand in 1976, this delightful miniature is extremely dwarf with tiny single light pink or white flowers with gold stamens. It is not hardy enough for planting outside in cooler climates. ◑ *

'Black Lace'. *C.* x *williamsii* 'Donation' x *C. reticulata* 'Crimson Robe', this camellia has proved remarkably hardy and reliable, flowering freely, mid-season to late, after quite severe British winters. It has medium-sized dark red formal double flowers with in-curved petals and a velvety sheen, only rarely producing the marginal black lace effect. When it does it is a sight to behold! It forms a compact upright bush with dark green glossy leaves. It originated in 1971 in Mississippi. USA. ○◑● ***

'Blissful Dawn'. Another 'Donation' x *reticulata* seedling, bred in New Zealand, and registered in 1982, but this time the pollen parent is thought to be 'Wild Retic'. It is a lovely shade of pink with white or pale pink bases to the petals of the medium to large, semi-double flowers which appear in mid-season. Its habit is upright and open in a rigid sort of way. It appears to be hardy in Britain, but has not yet had a really hard winter to test it. ◑ **

'California Dawn'. A *C. sasanqua* x *C. reticulata* hybrid, which flowers early in spring on an upright, vigorous, bushy plant. The flowers are large, light pink, semi-double to loose peony, with crinkled petals and quite freely produced. It was introduced by the Nuccio's nursery in 1987. ◑ **

'Cinnamon Cindy'. *C. japonica* x *C. lutchuensis*. Bred by Bill Ackerman in Maryland and introduced in 1974, this is named because its fragrance is described as deep cinnamon. The miniature peony form blooms have white petaloids mixed with

orange anthers and white filaments to the stamens, with rose pink outer petals . A most attractive flower which blooms early to late on an upright bush of moderate vigour. It is not fully tested outside in the UK yet, but certainly makes an excellent plant for the conservatory. ◑ *

'Cornish Snow'. A *C. cuspidata* x *C. japonica* hybrid, it was raised at Caerhays Castle in Cornwall, by J.C. Williams but is said to have started its commercial life with the well known Dorset nurseryman Jimmy Marchant who is said to have rooted a sprig of 'Cornish Snow', given to him for his button hole while a house guest of the Williams family. 'Cornish Snow' eventually makes a large spreading bush which produces masses of miniature flowers which are white with a slight pink flush, over a long period from early to late. Young growth is bronze. ○◑● ***

'Cornish Spring'. *C. cuspidata* x *C. japonica*, bred by Gillian Carlyon at Tregrehan in Cornwall, this hybrid was introduced in 1973. It is very different to 'Cornish Snow', having small to miniature, bright pink, single flowers on a slow growing, bushy upright plant. The bronze young growth is attractive. The flowers fade rapidly in sunny sites. ◑ **

'Dream Girl' *C. sasanqua* x *C. reticulata* . Originated by Howard Asper of California, and introduced in 1966 this, together with the other two 'Girls' was something of a breakthrough in hybridising at the time. The flowers are large, like its *reticulata* parent 'Buddha', semi-double with wavy, light pink petals. It is slightly scented like its *sasanqua* parent 'Narumigata'. It flowers in midwinter on a strong upright bush. ◐◑ **

'El Dorado' (*C. pitardii* x *C. japonica* 'Tiffany'). From Howard Asper in California, registered in 1968. Appreciated because of its very soft pink colouring and its ability to flower very freely; its flowers are medium to large, open peony form with creped and notched petals, mid-season. The bush is upright, vigorous, with mid green, slightly matt-textured leaves. ◑ **

'Fairy Wand'. *C. saluenensis* x *C. japonica* crossed with 'Tiny Princess' (*C. japonica* x *C. fraterna*), by Oz Blumhardt in New Zealand, registered in 1982. This useful miniature has bright rose pink semi-double flowers on an open upright plant of medium growth, in mid-season. As with so many *fraterna* hybrids the flowers are borne all along the branches in the axils of the leaves. ◑ **

'Felice Harris'. (*C. sasanqua* 'Narumigata' x *C. reticulata*), bred by Howard Asper of California, and introduced in 1961, this very very pale pink medium-sized semi-double is popular with professional landscape designers, for shady gardens as an alternative to a white choice (rather like choosing magnolia paint for a wall). It flowers mid-season on a vigorous upright bush which is slightly open in habit. ◑● **

'Flower Girl' (*C. sasanqua* 'Narumigata x *C. reticulata* 'Damanao') 1966. The second of 'The Girls', this one is a rich, yet soft, pink, large and with wavy petals which tend to recurve, giving the flowers an informal appearance. ◐◑ **

'Fragrant Pink'. (*C. rusticana* x *C. lutchuensis*). Originated by Dr Bill Ackerman in the USA

and introduced in 1966 this produces bright pink, miniature, peony-form blooms early to mid-season. The bush is vigorous, spreading and has small, light green leaves, which are bronze when young. Despite its *lutchuensis* parentage, it is quite hardy in southern England, but the scent is better under glass. The 'Fragrant Pink Improved' form is a more fertile one, (useful for hybridisers working for fragrance), produced by colchicine treatment, not a significant improvement in any other way. ◐◑ **

'Inspiration'. (*C. reticulata* Wild Form x *C. saluenensis*), originated at Exbury Gardens, England and first publicised in 1954, this is one of the most rewarding of landscape camellias. It flowers from early to late season on an upright, dense bush with lovely, neat, dark green glossy leaves. The flowers are medium-sized, phlox pink semi-doubles with the occasional petaloid, and are produced in great profusion. ◐◑● ***

'Itty Bit' (*C. saluenensis* x *C.* hybrid 'Tiny Princess'). This delightful miniature first flowered for its breeder, Felix Jury, in New Zealand in 1981 and has soft pink, anemone form flowers on a slow spreading bush. It is said to be hardy down to -10ºC. ◑ **

'Leonard Messel' (*C. reticulata* x *C.* x *williamsii* 'Mary Christian'). Large pink semi-double flowers with slightly deeper shading, this is a mid to late season variety which succeeds in cold climates. The bush is open and upright with strong rigid branches and matt, dark green leaves. ◐◑● ***

'Nicky Crisp' (*C. pitardii* x *C. japonica*). Raised by Bettie Durrant in New Zealand and named after her daughter, this is a highly successful variety, especially for small gardens in cold areas. It covers itself with flowers from early to late, they last well, then fall cleanly when finished. The blooms are clear pink, semi-doubles with golden stamens on a compact, slow growing bush with dark green leaves. ○◐● ***

'Night Rider' (hybrid 'Ruby Bells' x 'Kuro-tsubaki'), this was originated by Oz Blumhardt in New Zealand first flowered in 1980. The flowers are semi-double, with very dark red, heavy textured petals with stamens which have yellow anthers and reddish filaments. It forms an upright, tidy bush with small, dark green leaves with a reddish cast, which are a shiny purple red when young. 'Night Rider' is shy to flower in Britain, but is worth growing for its foliage and possible flowers in positions of warmth and good light. ◐ **

'Quintessence' (*C. japonica* x *C. lutchuensis*). Raised by John Lesnie in New Zealand and first introduced in 1985, this has a pronounced perfume from its dainty, white, miniature flowers which flower from early to late. It has slow spreading growth with tiny leaves. Ideal for trailing or for hanging baskets. ○◐ *

'Scented Sun'. A complicated hybrid with a large proportion of *C. japonica*, this was originated by Ken Hallstone in California in 1985. It has large, white, semi-double flowers with a very occasional pink stripe, with golden stamens and the occasional rabbit ears, early to mid-season. It has a good apple blossom fragrance. The bush is vigorous and upright with dark green leaves. ◐ **

'Show Girl'. (*C. Sasanqua* 'Narumigata' x *C. reticulata* 'Damanao', raised by Howard Asper in California and released in 1966. Similar to the other 'Girls', but has paler, later flowers. ○◐ **

'Spring Festival' (*C. cuspidata* hybrid of unknown parentage). This first bloomed in 1970 for its breeder Toichi Domoto in California, and has proved popular around the world, being particularly narrow and upright in its habit, and very free flowering in warm sites. It has delightful, miniature, rose form, double flowers of medium pink in mid to late season. The young growth is bronze. ○◐ **

'Spring Mist' (*C. japonica* 'Snow Bells' x *C. lutchuensis*). Originated by A.E. Longley and C.R. Parks (Dr Clifford R. Parks) in Los Angeles, this was first publicised in the *American Camellia Yearbook* in 1982. It has masses of dainty, very pale pink, semi-double flowers with a sweet perfume, blooming over a long period from early to mid-season. Growth is slow and spreading, with small mid-green leaves and coppery young growth. ◐ *

'Sweet Emily Kate'. (*C. japonica* 'Tiffany' x 'The Czar' x *C. lutchuensis*.) Bred by Ray Garnett in Victoria, Australia and first publicised in 1987, this sweetly scented miniature has informal tight peony form flowers of light pink shading to paler pink at the centre, with fluted petals, blooming in mid-season on a slow growing bush with a pendulous habit. ◐ *

Higo camellia 'Shintsukasa-nishiki'

'Tiny Princess' (*C. japonica* 'Akebono' x *C. fraterna*). First publicised in the USA in 1961, bred by K. Sawada in Alabama, this miniature has been very useful as a parent in hybridising programmes. It has tiny semi-double to loose peony flowers of white shading to delicate pink in mid-season. The leaves and habit are similar to *C. fraterna* but it is a little more hardy. ◑ **

'Yoimachi' (*C. sasanqua* 'Narumigata' x *C. fraterna*). Originated by Dr Clifford Parks of North Carolina and first publicised in 1982, this is a very early spring flowering miniature which, so far, flowers well outdoors after an average British winter and continues into mid-season. The flowers are single, white with pink shading on an upright bush which is open as a young plant but becomes dense as it matures. ◐◑ **

Some varieties to grow against sunny walls

C. sasanqua varieties: 'Bonanza', 'Dazzler', 'Narumigata', 'Plantation Pink', 'Shishigashira' (both tall and low growing forms), 'Sparkling Burgundy'. *reticulata* hybrids: 'Dream Girl', 'Flower Girl', 'Francie. L', 'Show Girl'. Some to grow against semi-shady walls: 'Captain Rawes', 'Dr Clifford Parks', 'Francie. L', 'Royalty'. *japonicas*: 'C.M. Hovey', 'Grand Prix'. *williamsii* varieties: ' Dream Boat', 'Joan Trehane', 'Waterlily'.

Some suggestions for shady walls: *williamsii* varieties: ' Daintiness', 'Elegant Beauty', 'Mary Phoebe Taylor', 'November Pink'.

SCENTED CAMELLIAS

There has been increasing interest in camellias which offer the added bonus of scented flowers. A number of the small-flowered, rather tender species are naturally scented, and some have been used in breeding programmes to produce fragrance in larger flowered hybrids. There are also some varieties of *C. japonica* which have a slight perfume reminiscent of carnations. Many of the Higo camellias also have fragrance, notably 'Nioi-Fubuki' and 'Okan'. Also some forms of *C. saluenensis*. *C. sasanqua* is another species which has scented forms and many scented varieties, with a somewhat pungent smell. Others which give pleasant fragrance outdoors in warm climates and under glass in cooler areas include *C. fraterna* (slight), *C.*

cooler areas include *C. fraterna* (slight), *C. forrestii*, *C. grijsii*, *C. kissñ*, *C. oleifera*, *C. tsaii*, *C. yuhsienensis* and *C. yunnanensis*. Some very handsome large-flowered forms of *C. yunnanensis* are now available, and *C. oleifera* has good sized blooms, but all the other species listed have small flowers and small leaves. Recently the beautiful *C. transnokoensis*, with its excellent, sweet, fragrance, tiny white flowers and little leaves, has come to prominence and there are hopes of some interesting hybrids from it. But it is *C. lutchuensis*, with its pleasant, sweet smell, which has featured most strongly in breeding for scent, combined with some of the scented *C. japonica* varieties.

The early work on breeding for fragrance started in the 1950s, in the USA, when *C. lutchuensis* was first obtained from Japan through the USDA. Howard Asper in California and Dr Bill Ackerman in Washington DC are credited with producing the first hybrids using this species, followed closely by seven crosses by Dr Clifford Parks working at that time in Los Angeles. Later, in the late 1960s and early 1970s, Dr Robert Cutter in Berkeley, California, joined Ackerman and Parks in a combined effort. Two hybrids with good scent and reasonably sized, anemone-form flowers resulted: 'Alice K. Cutter' and 'Virginia W. Cutter'. Bill Ackerman produced 'Fragrant Pink', and later 'Fragrant Pink Improved' (which, unlike its predecessor, has viable pollen). David Feathers, in Lafayette, California, produced two excellent hybrids: 'Apple Blossom' and 'Salab'.

Recent hybridisers with successful varieties now available include John Lesnie of New Zealand ('Quintessence') and Ray Garnett of Australia ('Sweet Emily Kate'), but the most active is undoubtedly Jim Finlay of New Zealand. He has introduced more than a dozen fragrant hybrids of good size and fragrance, most of which have strong *C. japonica* characteristics and should prove hardy enough for outdoors in most climates, with 'Superscent' probably one of the best. Most of Jim Finlay's hybrids are yet to become commercially available outside New Zealand, but those to watch out for are 'Superscent' – registered in 1987, a very full, deep peony form of good size with pale pink flowers shading to deeper pink at the petal margins as the flower ages; 'Master Scent', registered in 1993, a lovely light red full peony form with good foliage; 'Hyperscent', a rich red peony form which has won a 'Champion Bloom' award, regardless of its fragrance, which is good. There are several more on the way.

Camellia Nurseries And Gardens To Visit

Opening hours have not been given, nor have admittance fees to gardens as both change from time to time. Please telephone in advance to check.

AUSTRALIA

New South Wales-Sydney area:

Eryldene, 17, McIntosh Street, Gordon. NSW. Tel: 02 94982271. The home and garden of the late Professor Waterhouse, now run by a Trust. It is small but atmospheric and contains some interesting camellias, a Tea House and other Japanese features.
By appointment. A small fee is charged.

Camellia Grove Nursery. 240, Mona Vale Road, St Ives. Tel: 02 9144 3402. A compact garden nursery with plenty of well grown camellias and an excellent display of named blooms, cut fresh each day. Excellent, helpful small catalogue.

Paradise Plants, Greta Road, Kulnura 2250 NSW. Tel: 043 76 1330. This is a large wholesale nursery, from where the Paradise *sasanqua*s originate. The nursery and extensive gardens and arboretum are open for two weekends, only, one in early May to see the *sasanqua*s and one in late July or early August when hundreds of other mature camellias may be seen in flower in the 25-hectare gardens.

Cowell's Camellia Nursery, Terry Road, Theresa Park (via Camden) NSW. Tel: 046 512228. A popular place to visit, with mature plants in a garden setting. A good selection of varieties in all sizes.

Camellia Cottage (Three Bears) Nursery. 72, Castle Hill Road, West Pennant Hills. NSW 2125. Tel: 02 94843895. A very extensive range of varieties old and new.

Wagga Wagga Botanic Gardens. Contact The Wagga Wagga City Council, PO Box 20, Wagga Wagga. NSW. 2650 Tel: 069 235499. This is a 2.5-

C.j. 'Nuccio's Cameo'

hectare camellia garden section of the main gardens and contains hundreds of camellias planted since 1985, many of which were gifted by the Kunming Institute In China. Various Chinese buildings and features are included in the garden.

Victoria

Royal Botanic Gardens, Birdwood Avenue, South Yarra, Melbourne. Tel: 03 92522300. An extensive collection of camellias is included in the gardens which are well worth visiting.

Wodonga Plant Farm, run by the Pollard family at 6, Huon Creek Road, Wodonga, Victoria 3690. Tel: 060 245 561 A large list of camellias is available and the nursery has won many awards in the past.

South Australia

Newmans Nursery. North East Road, Tea Tree Gully, SA 5091. Tel: 08 82642661. A nursery with a very extensive range of camellias both old and

new varieties, and a pleasant hill side garden with mature camellias. Excellent catalogue which exudes enthusiasm and a desire to inform and help customers.

Western Australia

Pioneer Gardens Nursery. Cnr Lansdown Entrance and Nicholson Road, Canningvale 6155. Tel: 08 94551660. A very extensive collection of camellias including possibly 300 different *C. japonica* varieties, 50 to 60 *sasanqua* varieties, all well grown and good value.

GERMANY

Peter Fischer Gartenbau, Hoden 16 , 2177 Wingst. Germany. Tel: 04778 263. This nursery and gardens north east of Bremerhaven in northern Germany has a fine collection of camellias collected from all over the world. Peter Fischer has done much to assess these varieties for cold hardiness and is able to give sound advice.

C.j. 'Nuccio's Jewel'

C.j. 'Moonlight Bay'

FRANCE

Alain Stervinou, Kerguelen-29290 Guipronvel, France. Tel 02 98 07 28 00. Fax 02 98 07 20 99 This is a large wholesale nursery in Brittany, with a Garden Centre nearby. Good quality plants of about 150 camellia varieties, including many recent introductions, are available in a variety of sizes.

Pepinière Botanique & Plantarium de Gaujacq Jean and Fréderique Thoby, Chateau de Gaujacq, 40330 Gaujacq, France. Tel 05 58 89 24 22 Fax 05 58 89 06 62

This botanic nursery and garden in the far

southwest corner of France near Bayonne is a fairly new enterprise in the grounds of an old chateau. Nearly 400 species and cultivars of camellia are listed and many other plants of interest in an attractve' ancient document' style catalogue. There are over 600 varieties of camellia in the gardens. Open in the afternoons, daily except Wednesdays and over the Christmas period. Mail order available.

NEW ZEALAND

The Botanic Gardens of Auckland, Wellington, Christchurch and Dunedin all have good camellia collections.

Other gardens worth visiting include the following:

The Waipahihi Botanical Society's garden in Shepherd Road, Taupo.
    Pukeiti Rhododendron Trust. RD 4 New Plymouth.
    Pukekura Park, Private Bag, New Plymouth.
    Massey University Arboretum and Gardens. Palmerston North.

Camellia Haven, 80, Manuroa Road, Takanini. Near Auckland Tel: 9 298 7392. This is one of the best camellia nurseries, with a very extensive range of varieties and one of the best collections of Camellia species in the world available for purchase. It has an excellent display area and a concise catalogue. Scions may be exported overseas.

Lennards Nursery. State Highway 2. Papamoa, Bay of Plenty. Tel: 7 542 1215. An extensive range of camellias.

Mark Jury Nurseries. 591 Otaraoa Road, Tikorangi. RD 43 Waitara. North Taranaki. Tel: 6 754 8577
Mark, with his wife Abbie, is continuing the Jury family tradition of breeding new camellias and has an expanding nursery selling these and other camellias, magnolias and other plants, many of which are home bred.

UNITED KINGDOM

Antony Woodland Garden. Antony Road, Torpoint. Cornwall. PL11 2QA. Tel: 01752 814 355. A mature woodland garden which includes over 300 varieties of camellias . Open daily from 1st March to 31st October.

Caerhays Castle Garden, Caerhays, Gorran. St Austell . Cornwall. PL26 6LY.Tel: 01872 501 144 (recorded message). This is the garden, still owned by the Williams family, from which the first *williamsii* hybrids were raised. It does not have a vast collection of varieties, but is worth a visit in spring. Open mid March to early May weekdays only.

Marwood Hill Gardens and Nursery. Marwood Hill, Barnstaple. North Devon. Tel: 01271 42528. Dr Jimmy Smart's collection of camellias numbers over 1,000 species and cultivars mostly collected on his travels round the world. The gardens are open all year except Christmas Day.

Trehane Garden, Probus. Nr Truro. Cornwall TR2 4JG. Several hundred different camellia varieties, most of which were brought into Britain from overseas by David Trehane for trial in the British climate. The garden is open for charity on certain Sundays or by appointment. Tel: 0187 252 0270

C.j. 'Grand Prix'

Trewithen Gardens. Grampound Road, Nr Truro. Cornwall. TR2 4DD. Tel: 01726 883 647. A historic garden well known for its large specimen camellias and rare trees and shrubs many of which were wild collected. Open 1st March to 30th September (not Sundays except April and May.

Wentworth Castle Gardens, Stainborough, Barnsly, S Yorkshire. Tel 01226 731269
Extensive collection of camellias, with magnolias and species rhododendrons under a canopy of trees on a hillside at 1,000 feet. It is probably the best collection to be seen at such a northern latitude in such a hostile climate. A good place to see which camellias are truly cold hardy.

Nurseries
Coghurst Nursery. Ivy House Lane. Hastings. East Sussex TN35 4NP. Tel: 01424 756228. Specialist camellia nursery mostly selling through its exhibits at the RHS Shows in London and by mail order. Extensive catalogue, with many hard to find older varieties. Open daily all year except Saturdays.

C.j. 'Holly Bright'

C.j. 'Patricia Ann'

Stonehurst Nurseries. Selsfield Road, Ardingly, West Sussex RH17 6TN. Open daily and mail order, plus exhibits at RHS shows in London. Large selection, especially of varieties suitable for growing under glass for exhibition and competition. Open daily all year.

Trehane Nurseries. Stapehill Road, Hampreston. Nr Wimborne. Dorset. BH21 7NE. Tel: 01202 873490. Extensive selection of varieties and a few species. Full descriptive catalogue. Mail order and export. Not open at weekends except in peak flowering season in spring.

Camellia consultancy and 'Variety Search'. Jenifer Trehane Tel/Fax (UK) 01202 579368 (overseas) 44 1202 579368. E-mail jentrehane@compuserve.com

USA

California

Descanso Gardens. 1418 Descanso Drive, La Canada Flintridge. California 91012-0778. Tel: 818 952 4391. A large collection of mature camellias the 'camellia forest', many of which are of great

historic importance as they were the first C. *reticulata*s to be sent from Kunming, China to the USA. The Descanso Gardens Guild is a lively body which organises many camellia events and lectures to encourage a better understanding of the genus.

The Huntington Botanical Gardens, 1151 Oxford Road, San Marino, California 91108. Tel: 818 405 2100. One of the largest camellia collections in the USA planted in two of the gardens within the 130 acres.

The Nuccio's Nurseries, 3555 Cheney Trail, Altadena. Ca 91001. Tel: 818 794 3383. Probably the best camellia nursery in the world, with over 500 varieties and species for sale from immaculate premises. Comprehensive catalogue and mail order.

Georgia

The American Camellia Society Headquarters, One Massee Lane, Fort Valley, Georgia 31030. There are extensive gardens, and a headquarters building from which excellent information about camellias may be obtained. Open weekdays, daily. Also part weekends Nov 1st to March 31st. Tel: 912 967 2358.

North Carolina

Camellia Forest Nursery, 125 Carolina Forest Road, Chapel Hill. NC 27516. This is the nursery owned by Prof. Clifford Parks and run by his wife Kai-Mei and son. It specialises in hardy camellias and includes a number of new, home bred varieties. Open by appointment. Tel: 919 967 5529.

There are many more nurseries and some gardens throughout the USA. The American Camellia Society headquarters at Massee Lane should be able to help with addresses.

CAMELLIA SOCIETIES

The International Camellia Society exists to promote enjoyment, knowledge and understanding of camellias worldwide. The Society is also responsible for the registration of all new camellia cultivars and has published a 32,000-variety Register, with supplement. Members come from over 20 countries and meet every other year in a different country to hold a Congress, where papers are read and delegates meet to discuss camellia matters of interest at all levels. Gardens are visited, tours arranged, and the hospitality of the host country enjoyed. An excellent journal is published annually.

The Society does not, at the time of writing, have a permanent address, but information can usually be obtained by contacting camellia nurseries or gardens, or by visiting the ICS website through the internet.

The American Camellia Society, One Massee Lane. Fort Valley, Georgia 31030. Tel: 912 967 2358. In addition to the facilities of the headquarters members receive a full colour quarterly journal and a substantial *Yearbook*. New camellia varieties are fully described in their publications as they are registered.

The Southern California Camellia Society has long been active in the registration of new camellias and the production of the *Camellia Nomenclature* which will continue, as long as it is produced, to be an invaluable, concise guide to the identification of camellia cultivars and used throughout the world. The Society continues to be active in stimulating interest in camellias and has strong links with the Descanso Gardens Trust.

There are active National Societies in Australia, Japan, China and New Zealand and branches of the ICS which are also active within the Society at regional level within the countries of France, Germany, the UK and the Channel Islands.

THE INTERNET

The ICS has a web site through which information may be obtained or exchanged: http://www.med-rz.uni-sb.de/med_fak/physiol2/camellia/home.htm

The up-to-date names of all the membership representatives and their addresses may be obtained from this site, and much more is being added.

The same website gives information about other camellia societies and many more camellia matters.

There are facilities in most towns around the world where the Internet may be accessed, and the information printed out, for a small fee, if readers do not have the facility at home or work.

BIBLIOGRAPHY

The journals of:
The International Camellia Society
The American Camellia Society
The Australian Camellia Society
The Southern California Camellia Society
The New Zealand Camellia Society

Camellias. Chang & Bartholomew. Timber Press 1984
The Camellia Story. Tom Durrant. Heineman. 1982
The Colour Dictionary of Camellias. Stirling Macoboy. 1984
Camellias of China. China Esperanto Press. 1995.
The Yunnan Camellias of China. Kunming

Institute of Botany. Science Press.(Beijing) 1986.
5000 Years of Tea. Derek Maitland. Gallery Books 1982
Gardening with Camellias. Jim Rolfe. Godwit 1992
A Plantsman's Guide to Camellias. David Trehane. Ward Lock. 1990
A Revision of the Genus Camellia. J. Robert Sealy. Royal Horticultural Society. 1958
The International Camellia Register (compiled by Tom Savige) International Camellia Society. 1992
Camellias. Harold Hume. Macmillan. 1951
The Camellia- its History, Culture, Genetics and future development. The American Camellia Society. 1978

C. yuhsienensis

INDEX

This index includes all important entries and those mentioned more than once. The effectively self-indexing sections between pp134-172 are not included here. Bold location references refer to illustrations.

INDEX